The Lord and Churchill Family Genealogy

Phyllis Evelyn Lord with her grandfather Otis B. Churchill.
Maple Rock Farm, Parsonsfield, Maine

The Lord and Churchill Family Genealogy

DESCENDANTS OF NATHAN LORD OF KITTERY, MAINE

D. Kimball Lord
Theresa Churchill (Lord) Libby

Genealogy House Publishers
Amherst, Massachusetts

This is an update of an earlier version printed for the family by
Theresa Churchill (Lord) Libby in1969

ISBN: 978-1-887043-40-3

Published by Genealogy House, a division of White River Press, PO Box 3561, Amherst, MA 01004

Photo credits: Engravings of Elisha Wadleigh, Elisha Wadleigh, Jr. Elisha S. Wadleigh from *A History of the First Century of the Town of Parsonsfield, Maine;* Mary Banks sampler and postcard of Maple Rock Farm from the Treworgy family collection; portrait of Phyllis, photo by Martha T. Harris. All other farm photos from the collection of Theresa Churchill Lord. Negatives developed by Dave Williams.

Cover photos: Maple Rock Farm (front) and Treworgy House (back) by Martha T. Harris

Library of Congress Cataloging-in-Publication Data

Names: Lord, D. Kimball, 1965- author. | Libby, Theresa Churchill Lord,
    author.
Title: The Lord and Churchill family genealogy : descendants of Nathan Lord
    of Kittery, Maine / D. Kimball Lord, Theresa Churchill (Lord) Libby.
Other titles: Descendants of Nathan Lord of Kittery, Maine
Description: Amherst, Massachusetts : Genealogy House Publishers, [2018] |
    Includes index.
Identifiers: LCCN 2018021713 | ISBN 9781887043403 (hardcover : alk. paper)
Subjects: LCSH: Maine--Geneaology. | Lord family. | Churchill family. | Lord,
    Nathan, 1630-1690--Family. | Maine--Biography.
Classification: LCC F18 .L86 2018 | DDC 929.20973--dc23
LC record available at https://lccn.loc.gov/2018021713

Contents

Introduction vii

Part One: Descendants of 1

NATHAN LORD & JUDITH CONLEY 3

JOHN CHURCHILL & HANNAH PONTUS 15

THOMAS SMITH CHURCHILL, JR & MARY ANN DIXON 35

OTIS BANKS CHURCHILL & SUSAN E FERREN 38

JOHN C CHURCHILL & ANNIE BURK 50

MARY RELIANCE CHURCHILL & NEHEMIAH TOWLE LIBBY 52

Part Two: Biographies, stories, and reminiscences 55

NATHAN LORD 57

JOSEPH MERRILL LORD 58

WILBUR LORIN MERRILL 66

YANKEE INGENUITY IN ENGINEERING 72

ELISHA WADLEIGH, SR 76

ELISHA WADLEIGH, JR 77

ELISHA SMITH WADLEIGH 78

Major THOMAS AND MARY CHURCHILL 79

PHYLLIS EVELYN (LORD) TREWORGY 81

Part Three: Maple Rock Farm 87

MAPLE ROCK FARM c.1799 89

Notes 127

Index 129

Introduction

Nathan Lord was a young child when he and his family sailed from the county of Kent in England to Kittery, Maine in 1638. As a grown man he eventually acquired substantial amounts of land in and around what is known as Eliot, Maine.

Thanks to Nathan Lord's descendants, Theresa Lord Libby, David Lord, and D. Kimball Lord, the details compiled here are an accurate genealogical line of Nathan. Theresa initially spent many hours on her typewriter making carbon copies of her information. David added to these details with more research. Finally D. Kimball Lord, (Kim) for thirty years has devoted much of his time researching, compiling and organizing this information.

Linda Treworgy Faatz
Gorham, Maine
May 2018

Part One:
Descendants of...

DESCENDANTS OF NATHAN LORD & JUDITH CONLEY

1. **Nathan Lord** (A, B) (b. 1630 In Rye, Sussex, Kent County, England d. December 24, 1690) Nathan settled in Kittery, ME on land granted him there on December 16, 1652 & on April 28, 1653 married **Judith Conley**, his step-sister (b. 1632 d. 1658) daughter of Abraham & Elizabeth Conley. His father-in-law, Abraham Conley came from Kent to Kittery as early as 1637 & on March 1, 1674 willed to Nathan his Sturgeon Creek land, except the part that he had granted to Francis Small in an inventory dated March 18, 1677-8. Nathan married **Martha Everett** in 1678 (Martha was Judith's step-sister). Nathan & Judith had 3 children. Nathan & Martha had 6 children:

2. Nathan II	b. March 28, 1655	d. September 24, 1733
2. Abraham	b. 1657	d. May 11, 1705
2. Samuel	b. 1658	d. November 20, 1689
2. Martha	b. 1660	d.
2. Margery	b. 1672	d. April 26, 1703
2. Sarah	b.	d.
2. Ann	b.	d.
2. Mary	b.	d. July 16, 1696
2. Benjamin	b. 1685	d. 1745

2. **Nathan Lord II** on November 22, 1678 married **Martha Tozier** (b. 1657 d. 1758) daughter of Richard & Judith (Smith) Tozier; Martha 42 years old in document of January 23, 1682. Nathan acquired parcels of land, Berwick-Kittery Area, 1676-97. They had 11 children:

3. Martha	b. October 14, 1679	d.
3. Nathan III	b. May 13, 1681	d.
3. William	b. March 20, 1683	d. 1741
3. **Richard (Captain)**	b. March 1, 1685	d. 1754
3. Judith	b. March 20, 1687	d. January 31, 1776
3. Samuel	b. June 14, 1689	d. May 19, 1762
3. Mary	b. July 29, 1691	d.
3. John	b. January 19, 1693	d. 1761
3. Sarah	b. March 28, 1696	d.
3. Anne	b. May 27, 1697	d.
3. Abraham **(Captain)**	b. October 29, 1699	d. April 8, 1779

3. **Richard Lord** (Captain) In December 1707 married **Mary Goodwin** (b. May 23, 1691 d. 1763) daughter of James & Sarah (Thompson) Goodwin. They had 13 children:

4. Richard	b. November 23, 1708	d. 1754
4. **James (Sergeant)**	b. February 24, 1711	d. 1772
4. Moses	b. January 24, 1713	d. Before 1754
4. Aaron	b. January 27, 1715	d.
4. Sarah	b. December 28, 1716	d. Before 1754
4. Nathan IV	b. December 5, 1718	d.
4. Adam	b. January 6, 1721	d. Before 1754
4. Mary	b. January 17, 1723	d. Before 1754
4. Amy	b. November 26, 1724	d. 1750
4. Keziah	b. November 26, 1726	d. December 6, 1802
4. Joseph	b. July 26, 1728	d. April 15, 1802
4. Meribah	b. May 3, 1730	d.
4. Jabez	b. June 25, 1732	d. 1799

4. **James Lord** (Sergeant/Soldier in The French Indian War) In 1732 married **Sarah Stone Libby** (b. February 2, 1713 d. After 1755) daughter of Deacon Benjamin & Sarah (Stone) Libby. The children were baptized in South Berwick between 1735-55. They had 13 children:

5. James	b. August 26, 1733	d.
5. Sarah	b. November 9, 1735	d. June 30, 1770
5. Mary	b. June 10, 1737	d. In Infancy
5. Richard	b. October 8, 1738	d.
5. Lydia	b. October 18, 1740	d.
5. Jeremiah	b. August 29, 1742	d.
5. Anna	b. February 24, 1744	d.
5. Jacob	b. March 13, 1746	d.
5. **Adam**	b. December 20, 1747	d. 1782
5. Mary	b. August 22, 1749	d. October 23, 1824
5. Keziah	b. August 16, 1751	d.
5. Daniel	b. May 26, 1753	d.
5. Benjamin	b. December 2, 1755	d. In Infancy

5. **Adam Lord** on April 30, 1771 married **Olive Knight** (b. May 1753 d. July 8, 1827) in Berwick, ME. Adam served in Captain James Littlefield's Company, Colonel Storer's Regiment. He died as a Revolutionary War Soldier from small pox. Adam served as a Private in the Penobscot Expedition & at Burgoyne's Surrender in 1775. In 1790 Olive married George Stone & she lived in Limington with her sons John & James. Son James filed an affidavit of service on September 28, 1846. They had 2 children:

6. **John**	b. March 29, 1772	d. April 9, 1843
6. James	b. March 15, 1774	d. December 3, 1848

6. **John Lord** (C, D, E) on January 24, 1796 married **Eunice Libby** (b. January 31, 1774 d. May 29, 1843) daughter of Daniel & Lois (Jones) Libby of Berwick, ME. Eunice was born as a twin to James Libby. They had 5 children:

7. Olive	b. July 31, 1797	d. March 11, 1843
7. James	b. June 28, 1799	d. November 25, 1873
7. George	b. July 10, 1802	d. January 1865
7. Phebe M	b. November 7, 1803	d. April 6, 1876
7. **Daniel**	b. June 17, 1810	d. June 10, 1877

7. **Daniel Lord** on February 13, 1834 married **Louisa McKenney** (b. December 1, 1812 d. September 4, 1862) of Limington, ME. They had 1 child:

8. Harriet Newell	b. April 25, 1838	d. November 28, 1855

Daniel on February 23, 1863 married **Josephine Burbank Merrill** (H)
(b. December 15, 1824 d. October 25, 1894) daughter of Joseph & Hannah E (Burbank) Merrill. They had 2 children:

8. **Joseph Merrill**	b. October 29, 1865	d. February 27, 1920
8. Hattie Julia	b. March 28, 1868	d. April 8, 1890

Josephine on July 3, 1879 married **Elisha Smith Wadleigh** (F) (b. December 6, 1830 d. June 26, 1912) son of Elisha Wadleigh, Jr & Mary A Burbank of Parsonsfield, ME.
Josephine & Elisha had no children.

8. **Harriet Newell Lord** never married or had children

8. **Joseph Merrill Lord** on August 30, 1893 married **Sarah May Churchill** (b. June 14, 1865d. December 20, 1934) daughter of Otis Banks & Susan E (Ferren) Churchill of N Parsonsfield, ME. They had 5 children:

9. Theresa Churchill	b. November 27, 1894	d. June 26, 1969
9. Frank Wadleigh	b. January 3, 1897	d. February 21, 1979
9. Myron Otis	b. January 19, 1899	d. July 17, 1951
9. Daniel Bertram	b. September 18, 1901	d. September 25, 1959
9. Phyllis Evelyn	b. May 27, 1909	d. December 30, 2002

8. **Hattie Julia Lord** on November 9, 1887 married **Arthur Louis Strout** (b. December 31, 1866 d. June 14, 1893) son of Reverend Thomas & Rachel (Hicks) Strout of N Parsonsfield, ME. They had 1 child:

9. Hattie Lula	b. June 14, 1888	d. January 2, 1974

9. **Theresa Churchill Lord** on January 22, 1921 married **Donald Maxwell Libby** (b. September 26, 1896 d. March 29, 1972) son of Frank Willard & Elizabeth (Philpot) Libby of Limerick, ME. They had 2 children:

10. Kathryn Churchill	b. May 27, 1922	d. December 1, 1994
10. Joanne Elizabeth "Jose"	b. August 13, 1926	d.

9. **Frank Wadleigh Lord** on September 17, 1919 married **Ruth Doris Verbeck** (b. January 1, 1895 d. January 20, 1980) daughter of Calvin Maurice & Ida Susan (Hadlock) Verbeck of Malden, MA. They had 3 children:

10. Jay Merrill	b. July 28, 1921	d. August 13, 1987
10. Howard Verbeck	b. March 8, 1924	d. August 8, 2013
10. Philip Wadleigh	b. February 4, 1926	d.

9. **Myron Otis Lord** on August 9, 1924 married **Edith Josephine Sweeney** "Jo" b. January 25, 1899 d. April 28, 1975) daughter of Timothy & Eliza Jane (Gilliam) Sweeney of Phippsburg, ME. Myron & Edith had no children.

9. **Daniel Bertram Lord** on December 26, 1930 married **Irene Stanley** (b. November 26, 1909 d. October 6, 1986) daughter of Everett George & Elma (Tarbox) Stanley of Kezar Falls, ME. They had 2 children:

10. Ann	b. September 20, 1931	d. February 13, 2005
10. David Merrill	b. December 16, 1936	d.

9. **Phyllis Evelyn Lord** on July 2, 1936 married **Audway Stuart Treworgy** "Stubby" (b. March 30, 1907 d. February 28, 1999) son of Paul Wilfred & Edith Sophia (Newcomb) Treworgy of Augusta, ME. They had 3 children:

10. Linda	b. November 23, 1942	d.
10. Martha	b. May 5, 1944	d. February 26, 2013
10. John Stuart	b. May 26, 1947	d.

9. **Hattie Lula Strout** on June 29, 1914 married **Leon Ellsworth Kendall, Sr.** (b. July 26, 1886 d. January 7, 1957) son of Gowen Frank & Lena (Smith) Kendall of Rockland, MA. They had 1 child:

10. Leon Ellsworth, Jr.	b. September 24, 1920	d. November 6, 2005

10. **Kathryn Churchill Libby** on August 23, 1947 married **Frank Hammond Tucker** (b. December 29, 1923 d. January 26, 2017) son of Frank Edmund & Evalyn V. (Godfrey) Tucker of Wilmington, DE. They had 3 children:

11. Elizabeth Godfrey "Libby"	b. November 29, 1948	d.
11. Sarah Lowell	b. April 18, 1951	d.
11. Margaret Sayre	b. September 8, 1954	d.

10. **Joanne Elizabeth Libby** "Jose" on June 23, 1948 married **David Ware Hays** (b. August 1, 1926 d. June 1, 1969) son of James McFadden & Rena Victoria (Green) Hays of Cape Elizabeth, ME. They had 3 children:

11. Susan Seabury	b. September 26, 1956	d.
11. David Libby "Buzz"	b. August 22, 1958	d.
11. Daniel McGowan	b. September 20, 1961	d. June 28, 2007

Joanne on April 29, 1995 married **Rev Fred Ingraham Glover** (b. June 13, 1924 d. April 28, 1996) son of John W Sr & Edith (Ingraham) Glover of Bangor, ME. Joanne & Fred had no children.

10. **Jay Merrill Lord** on November 13, 1943 married **Barbara Jane Appleton** "Bobbie" (b. July 21, 1920 d. July 31, 1993) daughter of Nelson Winfield & Caroline Stella (Metzger) Appleton of Jenkintown, PA. They had 3 children:

11. Nancy Carol	b. September 10, 1944	d.
11. Susan Diane	b. April 24, 1950	d.
11. Donna Jeanne	b. September 13, 1955	d.

10. **Howard Verbeck Lord** on August 16, 1945 married **Marilyn Leatrice Stacy** (b. April 7, 1925 d.   ) daughter of Lawrence & Isabelle (Sawyer) Stacy of Kezar Falls, ME. They had 2 children:

11. Geoffrey Stacy "Geoff"	b. February 12, 1947	d.
11. Joseph Merrill "J Merrill"	b. April 26, 1949	d.

Howard & Marilyn divorced in May 1982.
Howard on October 19, 1982 married **Connie Elizabeth Rossborough** (b. October 19, 1948 d. December 18, 2014) daughter of Paris & Jane (Bryant) Rossborough of Biddeford, ME. Howard & Connie had no children & divorced in 1997.

10. **Philip Wadleigh Lord** on June 21, 1952 married **Mary Alberta Henderson** (b. November 8, 1929 d.   ) daughter of Roderick Raymond & Helen Dorothy "Dot" (Davis) Henderson of W. Baldwin, ME. They had 3 children:

11. Robyn Jeanne	b. February 21, 1954	d.
11. Dana Wadleigh	b. April 4, 1956	d.
11. Alan David	b. November 4, 1958	d.

10. **Ann Lord** on September 17, 1955 married **James Hall Bonney, MD** (b. September 5, 1927 d. October 27, 1994) son of Albert & Esther (Hall) Bonney of Bath, ME. They had 1 child:

11. Leigh Anne	b. July 15, 1958	d.

10. **David Merrill Lord** on June 20, 1959 married **Martha Ann Dodge** (b. March 28, 1937 d.   ) daughter of John Sinclair & Miriam Lucy (Wentworth) Dodge of Brentwood, NH. They had 3 children:

11. Jonathan Daniel "Jon"	b. July 4, 1960	d.
11. Jay Merrill II	b. October 19, 1963	d.
11. David Kimball "Kim"	b. April 20, 1965	d.

David & Martha divorced on February 23, 1984.

10. **Linda Treworgy** on August 24, 1968 married **Wright Everett Faatz** (b. March 4, 1943 d.   ) son of Dr. Gerald Almon & Avis Josephine (Williams) Faatz of Unity, ME. They had 2 children:

11. Nathan Andrew	b. December 26, 1971	d.
11. Justin Joshua	b. January 20, 1976	d.

Linda & Wright divorced on June 16, 1979.

10. **Martha Treworgy** on August 5, 1967 married **Eric Mark Pettengill** (b. April 24, 1940 d.   ) son of George Waldo & Esther (Quigg) Pettengill of Island Falls, ME. They had 2 children:

11. Robyn Dayle	b. January 8, 1968	d.
11. Jennifer Lord	b. October 28, 1969	d.

Martha & Eric divorced in March 1972.

Martha on June 24, 1979 married **Robert Hulbert Harris** (b. November 6, 1931 d. January 17, 2012) son of Reginald Hulbert & Alice Eugenia (Hupper) Harris of Portland, ME. Martha & Robert had no children & divorced on September 9, 1993.

10. **John Stuart Treworgy** on December 31, 1968 married **Linda Lou Roghaar** (b. September 11, 1947 d.   ) daughter of George Edward Sr & Florence (Bigelow) Roghaar of Arlington, MA. They had 2 children:

11. Sarah Churchill	b. February 18, 1969	d.
11. Hannah Bigelow	b. November 5, 1971	d.

John & Linda divorced on May 25, 1980.

John had 2 children by **Anne-Marie Barbara Aigner** (b. December 10, 1945 d.   ) daughter of Lucien Lazlo & Mady Anne (Lenard) Aigner

11. Samantha Lenard	b. February 12, 1981	d.
11. Adam Scott	b. September 15, 1984	d.

John on July 11, 1992 married **Patricia Cheryl Pedlow** (b. December 25, 1947 d.   ) daughter of Donald Ellis & Margaret Joan (Ford) Pedlow of Indianapolis, IN. She had 2 children in a past union.

11. Shalane Grace Flanagan	b. July 8, 1981	d.
11. Maggie Clare Flanagan	b. December 28, 1983	d.

10. **Leon Ellsworth Kendall, Jr** on October 29, 1948 married **Barbara May Hussey** (b. October 20, 1927 d. January 31, 1986) daughter of Ralph & Louise (Towle) Hussey of E. Parsonsfield, ME. They had 2 children:

11. Joseph Hussey	b. June 11, 1949	d.
11. Constance Louise	b. December 31, 1952	d.

Leon on November 4, 1989 married **Ruth Sarah Arsneault** (b. August 12, 1927 d.   ) daughter of George & Mildred (Thorne)Dearborn of Cornish, ME. Leon & Ruth had no children.

11. **Elizabeth Godfrey Tucker** on May 20, 1984 married **Geoffrey David Gould** (b. October 11, 1939 d.   ) son of David Winfield & Grace (Hendrickson) Gould of Minneapolis, MN. They had 1 child:

12. Peter Coryell	b. April 25, 1985	d.

11. **Sarah Lowell Tucker** on August 28, 1989 married **David John Owens** (b. February 1, 1941 d.   ) son of David C & Iona (Pomeroy) Owens of Utica, NY. Sarah & David had no children & divorced in 2001.

11. **Margaret Sayre Tucker** on June 23, 1978 married **William Charles Mitchell Jr** (b. September 7, 1952 d.   ) son of William Charles Sr & Helen (Yates) Mitchell of Louisville, KY. They had 3 children:

12. Andrew Russell	b. February 7, 1983	d.
12. Susan Anne	b. September 18, 1986	d.
12. Brian Thomas	b. September 11, 1989	d.

11. **Susan Seabury Hays** on May 31, 1980 married **Daniel James Whalen** (b. June 9, 1949 d.   ) son of David James & Virginia Frances (Evers) Whalen of Tomahawk, WI. They had 2 children:

12. James David	b. August 4, 1984	d.
12. Thomas Hopkins	b. December 12, 1987	d.

11. **David Libby Hays** on February 13, 2005 married **Anna Roth** (b. February 26, 1959 d.   ) daughter of Henry & Sylvia Ellen (Grossberg) Roth of S. Nyack, NY. They had 2 children:

12. Benjamin Maxwell	b. August 2, 2006	d.
12. Will McGowen	b. August 2, 2006	d.

11. **Daniel McGowan Hays** on February 19, 1984 married **Ludmila Borisovna** (b. June 7, 1956 d.   ) daughter of Boris Alexendrovich & Nina Nikolaevna (Ukhova) Borisovna of Leningrad, USSR. Daniel & Ludmila had no children & divorced in November 1991.

11. **Nancy Carol Lord**

11. **Susan Diane Lord** on August 30, 1969 married **David Alan Dixon** (b. August 18, 1940 d. September 2, 1982) son of Ralph Edwin & Ruth (Conley) Dixon of Battle Creek, MI. They had 3 children:

12. Diane Lynne	b. December 19, 1971	d.
12. Aimee Leigh	b. March 14, 1975	d.
12. Audre Ruth	b. October 14, 1981	d.

11. **Donna Jeanne Lord** on July 4, 1993 married **Joseph Hussey Kendall** (b. June 11, 1949 d.   ) son of Leon Ellsworth & Barbara May (Hussey) Kendall of Cornish, ME. He had 2 children in a previous union:

12. Ryan Joseph	b. October 12, 1983	d.
12. Angela Mae	b. October 6, 1986	d.

Donna Jeanne & Joseph had no children.

11. **Geoffrey Stacy Lord** on November 27, 1968 married **Janet Irene Jepson** (b. September 21, 1950 d.   ) daughter of Oscar Lester & Elaine (Parker) Jepson of Berwick, ME. Geoff & Janet had no children & divorced in June 1980.

Geoff on August 23, 1980 married **Ellen Douglas McCausland** (b. September 4, 1959 d.   ) daughter of Thomas & Jean (Black) McCausland of Monkton, MD. Geoff & Ellen had no children.

11. **Joseph Merrill Lord** on October 4, 1975 married **Susan Holly Ripley** (b. December 23, 1952 d. daughter of Claire Edward & Beverly Madeline (Weeks) Ripley of Sheepscot, ME. They had 1 child:

12. Josieda Marie "Sadie"	b. February 6, 1982	d.

J Merrill & Susan divorced in October 1991.

J Merrill on August 1, 1992 married **Candace Rogers** (b. April 18, 1960 d.   ) daughter of Theodore Alan & Jane (Allen) Rogers of Port Townsend, WA. They had 1 child:

    12. Calvin Ambrose   b. December 9, 1993   d.

J Merrill & Candace divorced in 1997.

    J Merrill on March 28, 1998 married **Shelley Gravino** (b. September 27, 1959 d.   ) daughter of Guido Dominec & Evelyn Ruth (Giardina) Gravino of Niagara Falls, NY. J Merrill & Shelley had no children.

11. **Robyn Jeanne Lord** on September 30, 1989 married **Richard Allen Austin** (b. August 16, 1956 d.   ) son of Richard Henry & Carol Jane (White) Austin of Nashua, NH. They had 2 children:

    12. Molly Lord   b. December 18, 1991   d.

    12. Max Philip   b. January 19, 1994   d.

Robyn & Richard divorced in 2001.

    Robyn on February 25, 2007 married **Paul Allen Nichols** (b. July 27, 1966 d.   ) son of George Allen & Martha Ann (Martin) Nichols of Rome, GA. Robyn & Paul had no children.

11. **Dana Wadleigh Lord** on December 11, 1993 married **Shirley Dagmar Zeisberg** (b. January 19, 1950 d.   ) from Germany. Dana & Shirley had no children.

11. **Alan David Lord** on December 29, 1990 married **Anne Clemens Hendershott** (b. July 8, 1959 d.   ) daughter of Charles & Jacquelynn (Vizzini) Hendershott of New Orleans, LA. Alan & Anne had no children & divorced on February 3, 1994.

    Alan on December 17, 1994 married **Margaret Knott** "Margi" (b. October 6, 1959 d.   ) daughter of Sydney Tucker Jr & Ruth Ellen (Senate) Knott of Barnstable, MA. Alan & Margaret had no children.

11. **Leigh Ann Bonney** on September 9, 2000 married **Larry Ritzhaupt** (b. March 10, 1949 d.   ) son of Delbert Samuel & Iva Louise (Britton) Ritzhaupt of Galion, OH. Leigh & Larry had no children.

11. **Jonathan Daniel Lord** on August 6, 1988 married **Jill Marie Christofferson** (b. April 1, 1955 d.   ) daughter of Robert Stanley & Grace Irene (Smith) Christofferson of Hibbing, MN. They had 1 child:

    12. Jonathan Daniel Jr. "Daniel"   b. March 6, 1989   d.

11. **Jay Merrill Lord II** on October 27, 1990 married **Priscilla Ann Sawyer** (b. March 14, 1962 d.   ) daughter of Jeremy Jason & Barbara (Harmon) Sawyer of Hampton, NH. They had 1 child:

    12. Calvin Merrill   b. December 22, 1992   d.

11. **David Kimball Lord**

11. **Nathan Andrew Fates** on June 10, 2000 married **Corey Patricia Pike** (b. January 19, 1973 d.   ) daughter of Kenneth Thorton & Paula Marie (Powers) Pike of South Portland, ME. They had 1 child:

    12. Sophia Sage   b. December 21, 2005   d.

Nathan & Corey divorced on December 8, 2017.

11. **Justin Joshua Faatz** on August 27, 2005 married **Sarah Rosalind Rogers** (b. May 31, 1975 d.   ) daughter of Scott Guy & Vicki Ray (Porter) Rogers of Unity, ME. They had 2 children:

12. Joshua Nicholas	b. April 22, 2007	d.
12. Anna Elizabeth	b. May 25, 2010	d.

11. **Robyn Dayle Pettengill** on September 25, 2004 married **Dana Violette** (b. November 6, 1965 d.   )son of Marcel Sr. & Roberta Jean (Paulsen) Violette, of Cumberland, ME Robyn & Dana had no children & divorced on August 16, 2017.

11. **Jennifer Lord Pettengill** on October 5, 1996 married **Jay Kenneth Banks** (b. August 5, 1964 d.   ) son of Harland William & Betty Lou (Dodge) Banks of Gorham, ME. They had 4 children:

12. Jackson Audway	b. June 1, 1999	d.
12. Georgia Elizabeth	b. January 12, 2001	d.
12. Griffin William	b. November 27, 2002	d.
12. Jay Hudson	b. April 24, 2008	d.

Jennifer & Jay divorced January 2, 2014.

11. **Sarah Churchill Treworgy** on June 29, 2002 married **John de LaChapelle** (b. October 15, 1961 d.   ) son of Richard Passerat & Patricia Ruth (Fisher) de LaChapelle of Oak Harbor, WA. They had 2 children:

12. Finn Stuart	b September 9, 2005	d.
12. Jack Edward	b. July 31, 2008	d.

11. **Hannah Bigelow Treworgy** on February 28, 2005 married **George Ekwere** (b. May 25, 1976 d.   ) son of Joseph Ekwere & Magrete Luma of Limbe, South West Province, Cameroon. They had 1 child:

12. Jasper Bigelow	b. June 24, 2009	d.

Hannah & George divorced November 4, 2016.

11. **Samantha Lenard Aigner-Treworgy**

11. **Adam Scott Aigner-Treworgy** on September 5, 2015 married **Susan Joyce Davis** (b. November 10, 1979 d.   ) daughter of Gerald Vincent & Anne Veronica (Torpey) Davis of Philadelphia, PA.

11. **Joseph Hussey Kendall** on October 27, 1979 married **Elizabeth Ann Bowen** (b. May 28, 1959 d.   ) daughter of James Vincent & Margorie Patricia (Sutton) Bowen of Rowley, MA. They had 2 children:

12. Ryan Joseph	b. October 12, 1983	d.
12. Angela Mae	b. October 6, 1986	d.

Joseph & Elizabeth divorced on November 9, 1989.
Joseph on July 4, 1993 married **Donna Jeanne Lord** (b. September 13, 1955 d.   ) daughter of Jay Merrill & Barbara (Appleton) Lord of Warminster, PA. Joseph & Donna Jeanne had no children.

11. **Constance Louise Kendall** on October 28, 1978 married **Douglas Burns Forbes Jr** (b. February 11, 1949 d.   ) son of Douglas Burns & Hazel (Estabrooks) Forbes of Kezar Falls, ME. They had 4 children:

12. Katie	b. March 2, 1980	d. May 15, 2005
12. Andrew	b. March 30, 1984	d.
12. Allison	b. July 20, 1986	d.
12. Alexander	b. July 20, 1986	d.

Constance & Douglas divorced February 2008.

12. **Peter Coryell Gould** on July 20, 2018 married **Elizabeth Anne Francis** (b. December 29, 1991 d.   ) daughter of John Leroy & Kelley (Sax) Francis of Johnson City, NH.

12. **Andrew Russell Mitchell** on April 17, 2013 married **Rebecca Catherine Riggs** (b. February 16, 1990 d.   ) daughter of Christopher Thomas & Glenda Rachel Hill (Evers) Riggs of Westcliffe, CO. They had 2 children:

13. Jack William	b. September 1, 2013	d.
13. Grace Tucker	b. June 28, 2016	d.

12. **Susan Anne Mitchell** on July 14, 2009 married **Matthew Joseph Miller** (b. January 4, 1987 d.   ) son of Mark Miller & Molly (Tate) Matheny of Nashville, TN. They had 1 child:

13. Lilly Anne	b. December 17, 2009	d.

12. **Brian Thomas Mitchell** on May 28, 2016 married **Lindsey Tenneson** (b. August 21, 1990 d.   ) daughter of

12. **James David Whalen**

12. **Thomas Hopkins Whalen** on August 8, 2014 married **Abby Louise Blinkhorn** (b. August 28, 1983 d.   ) daughter of William & Marilyn (Helena) Blinkhorn of Portland, ME

12. **Benjamin Maxwell Hays**

12. **Will McGowan Hays**

12. **Diane Lynne Dixon** on July 10, 1999 married **Donald Wesley Underwood** (b. November 10, 1971 d.   ) son of Donald Lloyd & Carolyn (Caldwell) Underwood of Gobles, MI. They had 2 children:

13. Gibson David	b. May 14, 2001	d.
13. Baxter Donald	b. July 22, 2006	d. July 22, 2006

12. **Aimee Leigh Dixon** had 1 child by **Ronald Dean Burgess** son of Ronald Elbert & Pauline Elizabeth (Lynch) Burgess of Nederland, CO

13. Sadira Nadine Burgess	b. August 7, 2000	d.

Aimee on September 18, 2010 married **Randall Mark Staples** (b. July 2, 1959 d.   ) son of Mark Paul & Jeaneen Atlantis (Senjem) Staples of Star Prairie, WI. Aimee & Randall had no children.

12. **Audre Ruth Dixon** on August 8, 2017 married **Ronald Raymond Rabb Jr** (b. May 4, 1981 d.   )
son of Ronald Raymond Sr & Suzanne Pearl (Moser) Rabb of Kalamazoo, MI They had 2 children:

    13. Lucius Raymond   b. December 4, 2011   d.

    13. Wyleigh Jay   b. September 20, 2013   d.

12. **Josieda Marie Lord** on July 7, 2018 married **Kyle Robert Pettit** (b. October 7, 1984 d.   ) son of Donald Richard & Jo Ann (Parker) Pettit of Santa Rosa, CA

12. **Calvin Ambrose Lord**

12. **Molly Lord Austin**

12. **Max Phillip Austin**

12. **Jonathan Daniel Lord, Jr**

12. **Calvin Merrill Lord**

12. **Sophia Sage Fates**

12. **Joshua Nicholas Faatz**

12. **Anna Elizabeth Faatz**

12. **Jackson Audway Banks**

12. **Georgia Elizabeth Banks**

12. **Griffin William Banks**

12. **Jay Hudson Banks**

12. **Finn Stuart de LaChapelle**

12. **Jack Edward de LaChapelle**

12. **Jasper Bigelow Ekwere**

12. **Ryan Joseph Kendall**

12. **Angela Mae Kendall**

12. **Katie Forbes** never married or had children.

12. **Andrew Forbes**

12. **Allison Forbes** had 1 child by **Ryan Travis Sargent** (b. November 5, 1982 d.   ) son of Rodney Lajoie & Cheryl Sargent of Standish, ME.

     13. Ryker Trig   b. May 24, 2012   d.

12. **Alexander Forbes**

12. **Jack William Mitchell**

12. **Grace Tucker Mitchell**

12. **Gibson David Underwood**

13. **Baxter Donald Underwood** never married or had children.

13. **Sadria Nadine Burgess**

13. **Lucius Raymond Rabb**

13. **Wyleigh Jay Rabb**

13. **Ryker Trig Sargent**

DESCENDANTS OF JOHN CHURCHILL & HANNAH PONTUS

1. **John Churchill** (E, I) b. 1620/4 d. January 1, 1663) on December 18, 1644 married **Hannah Pontus** (b. 1623 d. December 22, 1690) the daughter of William & Wybra (Hanson) Pontus of Plymouth, MA. They had 6 children:

2. **Joseph**	b. 1647	d.
2. Hannah	b. November 12, 1649	d. July 29, 1721
2. Eliezer	b. April 20, 1652	d. November 2, 1688
2. Mary	b. August 1, 1654	d.
2. William	b. 1656	d. October 5, 1722
2. John	b. 1657	d. June 13, 1723

   Hannah P Churchill married again on June 25, 1669 to **Giles Rickard/Reccord.** (b. 1623 d. November 3, 1688). Hannah & Giles had no children.

2. **Joseph Churchill** on June 3, 1672 married **Sarah Hicks** (b. 1649 d. November 2, 1688) daughter of Samuel & Lydia (Doane) Hicks of Plymouth, MA. They had 5 children:

3. John	b. July 3, 1678	d.
3. Margaret	b. October 1684	d.
3. **Barnabas**	b. July 3, 1686	d. May 24, 1760
3. Mercy	b. 1689	d. 1689
3. Joseph	b. January 1692	d.

3. **Barnabas Churchill** (E) on February 5, 1714 married **Lydia Harlow** (b. 1688 d. September 20, 1752) daughter of William & Lydia (Cushman) Harlow Plymouth, MA. They had 10 children:

4. Barnabas, Jr	b. October 19, 1714	d.
4. William	b. December 25, 1716	d.
4. Ichabod	b. January 12, 1719	d. October 1, 1745
4. Joseph	b. May 19, 1721	d.
4. Lemuel	b. July 12, 1723	d.
4. Isaac	b. May 3, 1726	d. 1761
4. **Thomas**	b. April 30, 1730	d.
4. Ebenezer	b. November 9, 1732	d.
4. Lydia	b. March 9, 1735	d.
4. John	b. May 9, 1739	d.

4. **Thomas** (E) on May 5, 1758 married **Mary Ewer** (b. August 7, 1737 d.   ) daughter of Nathaniel & Mary (Stewert) Ewer of Barnstable, MA. Thomas & Mary moved to Newmarket, NH after 1759. They had 11 Children:

5. Gamaliel	b. August 30, 1759	d. 1809
5. Polly	b. August 23, 1760	d.
5. Thomas	b. 1762	d. 1807
5. **Ichabod** (J)	b. June 24, 1764	d. September 15, 1855
5. Lydia	b. January 10, 1766	d.
5. Joseph	b. May 7, 1768	d. March 4, 1824
5. Susanna	b. August 18, 1770	d.
5. Nathaniel	b. March 31, 1772	d.
5. John I	b. 1774	d. 1774
5. John II	b. May 11, 1776	d.
5. Desire	b. March 27, 1778	d.

5. **Ichabod Churchill** (I) married **Elizabeth Doe** (b. 1769 d. November 23, 1809) daughter of Nicholas Jr. & Elizabeth (Sanborn) Doe. They had 6 children:

6. Nicholas	b. June 3, 1790	d. July 10, 1845
6. Elizabeth "Betsy"	b. March 27, 1793	d. March 30, 1877
6. John	b. September 22, 1795	d. October 5, 1873
6. **Thomas (Major)**	b. January 20, 1798	d. October 16, 1878
6. Mary "Polly"	b. January 24, 1801	d. May 17, 1865
6. Nancy	b. October 9, 1803	d. March 2, 1877

Ichabod on October 27, 1810 married **Leah Allen** (b. October 20, 1764 d. September 3, 1858)

6. **Thomas Churchill** (Major) on March 14, 1830 married **Mary Edgecomb Banks** (b. July 9, 1806 d. September 1, 1894) daughter of Jacob & Reliance (Edgecomb) Banks. They lived on The Churchill Farm. They had 8 children:

7. Thomas Smith Jr	b. May 6, 1831	d. April 9, 1919
7. Otis Banks	b. November 5, 1832	d. March 21, 1920
7. John C	b. December 11, 1834	d. May 9, 1923
7. Mary Reliance	b. February 12, 1837	d. February 18, 1930
7. Nathaniel H	b. May 8, 1839	d. March 15, 1922
7. Elizabeth Ann	b. August 21, 1841	d. March 17, 1844
7. Joseph	b. 1843	d. October 18, 1844
7. Lydia Frances	b. March 15, 1851	d. February 11, 1936

7. **Thomas Smith Churchill Jr** on January 1, 1855 married **Mary Ann Dixon** (b. October 2, 1832 d. December 30, 1878) daughter of William Dennett & Mary (Dearborn) Dixon of N Parsonsfield, ME. They had 3 children:

8. Eva	b. December 19, 1856	d. September 13, 1883
8. William Dennett Dixon	b. September 6, 1858	d. January 19, 1940
8. Thomas G	b. November 20, 1863	d. November 13, 1878

Thomas Jr on March 14, 1882 married **Olive Bowers Roberts** of Whitestown NY. Thomas & Olive had no children.

7. **Otis Banks Churchill** on January 2, 1861 married **Susan E Ferren** (b. January 14, 1838 d. January 7, 1911) daughter of James & Sally (Woodman) Ferren of Freedom, NH. They had 3 children:

8. Wilbur F	b. April 24, 1862	d. June 19, 1862
8. Charles Clarence	b. June 2, 1863	d. May 18, 1905
8. Sarah May	b. June 14, 1865	d. December 20, 1934

7. **John C Churchill** on October 18, 1869 married **Annie Burk** (b. September 5, 1846 d. February 22, 1917) daughter of William R & Ann Eulalie (Calbeck) Burk of E Boston, MA. They had 4 children:

8. Frank Percy	b. November 24, 1872	d. July 24, 1954
8. Preston Banks	b. April 21, 1876	d. September 22, 1956
8. Lindsey Walter	b. December 18, 1879	d. August 20, 1955
8. Eulalie	b. April 5, 1883	d. January 6, 1935

7. **Mary Reliance Churchill** on February 21, 1860 married **Nehemiah Towle Libby** (b. September 20, 1837 d. May 23, 1887) son of Isaac & Roxanna (Towle) Libby of Porter, ME. They had 2 children:

8. Emma A	b. November 2, 1862	d. 1892
8. Walter Day	b. November 8, 1864	d. August 6, 1941

7. **Nathaniel H Churchill** on January 7, 1885 married **Sophia Knapp Edgar** (b. 1843 d. 1925) of New York, NY. Nathaniel & Sophia had no children.

7. **Elizabeth Ann Churchill** never married or had children.

7. **Joseph Churchill** never married or had children.

7. **Lydia Frances Churchill** on May 5, 1880 married **John Washington Colcord** (b. September 26, 1849 d. November 7, 1885) son of Washington & Susan O Roberts Colcord of Porter, ME. (Colcord Pond Area) They had 1 child:

8. Lura Mildred	b. August 31, 1882	d. January 20, 1976

8. **Eva Churchill** in June 1, 1876 married **Joseph Boothby** (b. August 11, 1854 d. October 29, 1919) son of Samuel & Rebecca (Moulton) Boothby of Parsonsfield, ME. They had 1 child:

9. Lillian R "Birdie"	b. September 15, 1878	d. June 23, 1916

After Eva's death Joseph married again and moved to FL.

8. **William Dennet Dixon Churchill** on December 22, 1880 married **Clara Mabel Sweat** (b. September 14, 1859 d. April 12, 1900) daughter of Dr Moses E & Rebecca Sweat of N Parsonsfield, ME. They had 1 child:

    9. Harry William   b. December 29, 1884   d. November 16, 1937

8. **Thomas G Churchill** never married or had children.

8. **Wilbur F Churchill** never married or had children.

8. **Charles Clarence Churchill** on February 14, 1891 married **Ida Belle Chapman** (b. July 5, 1869 d. June 13, 1952) daughter of George Frank & Mary (Hussey) Chapman of N Parsonsfield, ME. They had 2 children:

    9. Lord Randolph   b. February 4, 1899   d. December 2, 1975
    9. Helen May   b. May 24, 1902   d. December 14, 1996

8. **Sarah May Churchill** on August 30, 1893 married **Joseph Merrill Lord** (b. October 29, 1865 d. February 27, 1920) son of Daniel & Josephine Burbank (Merrill) Lord of Parsonsfield, ME. They had 5 children:

    9. Theresa Churchill   b. November 27, 1894   d. June 26, 1969
    9. Frank Wadleigh   b. January 3, 1897   d. February 21, 1979
    9. Myron Otis   b. January 19, 1899   d. July 17, 1951
    9. Daniel Bertram   b. September 18, 1901   d. September 25, 1959
    9. Phyllis Evelyn   b. May 27, 1909   d. December 30, 2002

8. **Frank Percy Churchill** on July 16, 1899 married **Florence K Daniels** (b. 1870 d. 1950) daughter of Charles & Isabelle Daniels of Providence, RI. Frank & Florence had no children.

8. **Preston Banks Churchill** on October 3, 1900 married **Edythe Blaisdell** (b. November 22, 1876 d. February 26, 1964) daughter of Andrew M & Ella M (Crawford) Blaisdell of Brunswick, ME. They had 1 child:

    9. Lindsey Crawford   b. January 4, 1903   d. July 3, 1961

8. **Lindsey Walter Churchill** never married or had children.

8. **Eulalie Churchill** never married or had children.

8. **Emma A Libby** on January 30, 1887 married **Oscar F Wiggin** (b. 1857 d. July 4, 1887) son of Jacob & Rose A (Mason) Wiggin. Emma & Oscar F had no children.
    Emma in 1890 married **Edgar Francis Gentleman** (b. April 29, 1860 d. September 18, 1943) son of William Francis & Diana A (Wilkerson) Gentleman of Porter ME. They had 1 child:

    9. Merton Eugene   b. August 16, 1891   d. August 11, 1979

8. **Walter Day Libby** on June 16, 1889 married **Flora Lillian Hubbard** (b. October 22, 1871 d. March 19, 1937) daughter of Charles & Flora (Wadsworth) Hubbard of Hiram, ME. They had 2 children:

9. Harold Weston	b. August 17, 1892	d. April 9, 1972
9. Carleton Glen	b. February 6, 1894	d. November 26, 1956

8. **Lura Mildred Colcord** never married or had children.

9. **Lillian R Boothby** on December 12, 1897 married **Edgar Porter Jackson** (b. June 7, 1876 d. August 1, 1964) They had 1 child:

10. Lucille	b. 1899	d.

9. **Harry William Churchill** on November 20, 1910 married **Edna Anise Anderson** (b. March 19, 1886 d. November 7, 1972) daughter of William H & Annie (Morris) Anderson of Brooklyn, NY. They had 3 children:

10. Thomas William	b. June 27, 1913	d. December 8, 1979
10. Mabel Harriet	b. October 7, 1915	d. May 20, 2009
10. Ruth Louise	b. February 17, 1920	d.

9. **Lord Randolph Churchill** on October 16, 1926 married **Marguerite Grace Marston** (b. December 6, 1905 d. January 7, 1996) daughter of Dr. Clarence & Lula (Richardson) Marston of Brownfield, ME. They had 2 children:

10. Charles Clarence II	b. September 7, 1927	d. April 10, 2016
10. Robert Winston	b. June 12, 1930	d. May 4, 2008

9. **Helen May Churchill** on June 26, 1929 married **Verne McAllister Black** (b. July 19, 1902 d. August 5, 1988) son of Orion & Mabel (McAllister) Black of Kezar Falls, ME. They had 2 children:

10. James Orion	b. November 10, 1930	d. October 17, 2005
10. Laura Jane	b. August 23, 1932	d. February 24, 2017

9. **Theresa Churchill Lord** on January 22, 1921 married **Donald Maxwell Libby** (b. September 26, 1896 d. March 29, 1972) son of Frank Willard & Elizabeth (Philpot) Libby of Limerick, ME. They had 2 children:

10. Kathryn Churchill	b. May 27, 1922	d. December 1, 1994
10. Joanne Elizabeth "Jose"	b. August 13, 1926	d.

9. **Frank Wadleigh Lord** on September 17, 1919 married **Ruth Doris Verbeck** (b. January 1, 1895 d. January 20, 1980) daughter of Calvin & Ida Susan (Hadlock) Verbeck of Malden, MA. They had 3 children:

10. Jay Merrill	b. July 28, 1921	d. August 13, 1987
10. Howard Verbeck	b. March 8, 1924	d. August 8, 2013
10. Philip Wadleigh	b. February 4, 1926	d.

9. **Myron Otis Lord** on August 9, 1924 married **Edith Josephine Sweeney** "Jo" (b. January 25, 1899 d. April 28, 1975) daughter of Timothy & Eliza Jane (Gilliam) Sweeney of W Point, ME. Myron & Edith had no children.

9. **Daniel Bertram Lord** on December 26, 1930 married **Irene Stanley** (b. November 26, 1909 d. October 6, 1986) daughter of Everett George & Elma (Tarbox) Stanley of Kezar Falls, ME. They had 2 children:

10. Ann	b. September 20, 1931	d. February 13, 2005
10. David Merrill	b. December 16, 1936	d.

9. **Phyllis Evelyn Lord** on July 2, 1936 married **Audway Stuart Treworgy** "Stubby" (b. March 30, 1907 d. February 28, 1999) son of Paul Wilfred & Edith Sophia (Newcomb) Treworgy of Augusta, ME. They had 3 children:

10. Linda	b. November 23, 1942	d.
10. Martha	b. May 5, 1944	d. February 26, 2013
10. John Stuart	b. May 26, 1947	d.

9. **Lindsey Crawford Churchill** on January 29, 1929 married **Vieno Mary Kajander** (b. December 21, 1903 d. June 4, 1964) daughter on Jack & Mary (Laurila) Kajander of Fitchburg, MA. They had 2 children:

10. Lindsey Crawford Jr	b. August 10, 1935	d.
10. John Preston	b. October 30, 1939	d.

9. **Merton Eugene Gentleman** on July 13, 1924 married **Ava Magdalene Barnett** (b. March 5, 1898 d. July 6, 1991) daughter of William Skyler & Sarah (Fields) Barnett of Glen Elder, KS. They had 2 children:

10. Merton Eugene Jr	b. November 9, 1925	d.
10. Lawrence B	b. June 15, 1931	d. July 2, 2015

9. **Harold Weston Libby** on October 25, 1916 married **Marie Ona McClun** (b. April 11, 1893 d. September 23, 1925) daughter on John C & Elizabeth (Cribbs) McClun of Cawker City, KS. Harold & Marie had no children.

9. **Carleton Glen Libby** on September 4, 1920 married **Dorothy Elizabeth Norris** (b. February 5, 1896 d. November 25, 1991) daughter of Sidney Rendall & Maude (Whittelsey) Norris of Topeka, KS. They had 2 children:

10. Shirley Jeanne	b. October 7, 1922	d. March 5, 2002
10. Carolyn Lou	b. July 4, 1932	d.

10. **Lucille Jackson** never married or had children.

10. **Thomas William Churchill** never married or had children.

10. **Mabel Harriet Churchill** on October 25, 1947 married **Jesse Clinton Moran** (b. March 5, 1914 d. July 15, 1961) son of J Homer & Ada (Fuller) Moran of Manchester, GA. They had 4 children:

11. Ruth	b. October 14, 1948	d.
11. Thomas Olin	b. September 11, 1949	d. February 23, 1984
11. Julie	b. December 3, 1950	d.
11. Claire	b. March 27, 1952	d.

10. **Ruth Louise Churchill** on November 23, 1946 married **George Walter Weeks** (b. March 5, 1919 d. September 28, 1951) son of Howard E & Florence (Thornton) Weeks of E Parsonsfield, ME. They had 2 children:

11. Marshall Wendell	b. August 7, 1947	d.
11. Emily Susan	b. April 22, 1950	d.

Ruth on July 16, 1973 married **David Lester Jewell** (b. January 25, 1914 d.   ) son of John J & Emma Mae Jewell of Kezar Falls, ME. Ruth & David had no children.

10. **Charles Clarence Churchill II** on May 29, 1954 married **Nancy Ruth Dopp** (b. November 28, 1932 d.   ) daughter of Clarence Henry & Dorothy (Jenner) Dopp of Johnstown, NY. They had 2 children:

11. Susan Beth	b. July 15, 1958	d.
11. Steven Mark	b. April 26, 1960	d.

Charles & Nancy divorced in December 1969.
Charles on June 20, 1971 married **Nancy Jopp** (b. June 2, 1932 d. March 31, 2004) daughter of Kenneth & Evelyn Jopp of Delmar, NY. Charles & Nancy had no children & divorced on January 6, 1995.
Charles on August 18, 2013 married **Willa-Jo Mauger** (b. January 1, 1937 d.   ) daughter of Joseph Edward & Maxie Emma (Hopkins) Barricklow of Dabney, IN. Charles & Willa-Jo had no children.

10. **Robert Winston Churchill** on April 24, 1954 married **Dorothy Mae Leonard** (b. May 17, 1932 d.   ) daughter of Joseph Alfred & Susan (Moores) Leonard of Old Town, ME. They had 3 children:

11. Lynn Donna	b. July 1, 1955	d.
11. Dawn Linda	b. July 1, 1955	d.
11. Robert Alan	b. November 21, 1958	d.

10. **James Orion Black** on September 24, 1955 married **Charlotte Edwards** (b. December 1, 1934 d. November 21, 2007) daughter of Carroll & Eleanor (Bowie) Edwards of W Baldwin, ME. They had 3 children:

11. Cheryl Lee	b. January 28, 1961	d.
11. James Frederick	b. November 20, 1963	d.
11. John Carroll	b. December 19, 1964	d.

10. **Laura Jane Black** on February 5, 1954 married **Robert LeRoy Pike** (b. June 21, 1931 d. October 10, 2008) son of Robert Smith & Viola (Libby) Pike of Cornish, ME. They had 2 children:

11. Lorie Lee	b. January 16, 1957	d.
11. David Wyer	b. March 10, 1960	d.

10. **Kathryn Churchill Libby** on August 23, 1947 married **Frank Hammond Tucker** (b. December 29, 1923 d. January 26, 2017) son of Frank Edmund & Evalyn V. (Godfrey) Tucker of Wilmington, DE. They had 3 children:

11. Elizabeth Godfrey "Libby"	b. November 29, 1948	d.
11. Sarah Lowell	b. April 18, 1951	d.
11. Margaret Sayre	b. September 8, 1954	d.

10. **Joanne Elizabeth Libby** "Jose" on June 23, 1948 married **David Ware Hays** (b. August 1, 1926 d. June 1, 1969) son of James McFadden & Rena Victoria (Green) Hays of Cape Elizabeth, ME. They had 3 children:

11. Susan Seabury	b. September 26, 1956	d.
11. David Libby "Buzz"	b. August 22, 1958	d.
11. Daniel McGowan	b. September 20, 1961	d. June 28, 2007

Joanne on April 29, 1995 married **Rev Fred Ingraham Glover** (b. June 13, 1924 d. April 28, 1996) son of John W Sr & Edith (Ingraham) Glover of Bangor, ME. Joanne & Fred had no children.

10. **Jay Merrill Lord** on November 13, 1943 married **Barbara Jane Appleton** "Bobbie" (b. July 21, 1920 d. July 31, 1993) daughter of Nelson Winfield & Caroline Stella (Metzger) Appleton of Jenkintown, PA. They had 3 children:

11. Nancy Carol	b. September 10, 1944	d.
11. Susan Diane	b. April 24, 1950	d.
11. Donna Jeanne	b. September 13, 1955	d.

10. **Howard Verbeck Lord** on August 16, 1945 married **Marilyn Leatrice Stacy** (b. April 7, 1925 d.   ) daughter of Lawrence & Isabelle (Sawyer) Stacy of Kezar Falls, ME. They had 2 children:

11. Geoffrey Stacy "Geoff"	b. February 12, 1947	d.
11. Joseph Merrill "J Merrill"	b. April 26, 1949	d.

Howard & Marilyn divorced in May 1982.

Howard on October 19, 1982 married **Connie Elizabeth Rossborough** (b. October 19, 1948 d. December 18, 2014) daughter of Paris & Jane (Bryant) Rossborough of Biddeford, ME. Howard & Connie had no children & divorced in 1997.

10. **Philip Wadleigh Lord** on June 21, 1952 married **Mary Alberta Henderson** (b. November 8, 1929 d.   ) daughter of Roderick Raymond & Helen Dorothy "Dot" (Davis) Henderson of W Baldwin, ME. They had 3 children:

11. Robyn Jeanne	b. February 21, 1954	d.
11. Dana Wadleigh	b. April 4, 1956	d.
11. Alan David	b. November 4, 1958	d.

10. **Ann Lord** on September 17, 1955 married **James Hall Bonney**, MD (b. September 5, 1927 d. October 27, 1994) son of Albert & Esther (Hall) Bonney of Bath, ME. They had 1 child:

11. Leigh Anne	b. July 15, 1958	d.

10. **David Merrill Lord** on June 20, 1959 married **Martha Ann Dodge** (b. March 28, 1937 d.   )
daughter of John Sinclair & Miriam Lucy (Wentworth) Dodge of Brentwood, NH. They had 3 children:

11. Jonathan Daniel "Jon"	b. July 4, 1960	d.
11. Jay Merrill II	b. October 19, 1963	d.
11. David Kimball "Kim"	b. April 20, 1965	d.

David & Martha divorced on February 23, 1984.

10. **Linda Treworgy** on August 24, 1968 married **Wright Everett Faatz** (b. March 4, 1943 d.   ) son
of Dr. Gerald Almon & Avis Josephine (Williams) Faatz of Unity, ME. They had 2 children:

11. Nathan Andrew	b. December 26, 1971	d.
11. Justin Joshua	b. January 20, 1976	d.

Linda & Wright divorced on June 16, 1979.

10. **Martha Treworgy** on August 5, 1967 married **Eric Mark Pettengill** (b. April 24, 1940 d.   ) son
of George Waldo & Esther (Quigg) Pettengill of Island Falls, ME. They had 2 children:

11. Robyn Dayle	b. January 8, 1968	d.
11. Jennifer Lord	b. October 28, 1969	d.

Martha & Eric divorced in March 1972.
Martha on June 24, 1979 married **Robert Hulbert Harris** (b. November 6, 1931 d. January 17, 2012)
son of Reginald Hulbert & Alice Eugenia (Hupper) Harris of Portland, ME.
Martha & Robert had no children & divorced on September 9, 1993.

10. **John Stuart Treworgy** on December 31, 1968 married **Linda Lou Roghaar** (b. September 11, 1947
d.   ) daughter of George Edward Sr & Florence (Bigelow) Roghaar of Arlington, MA. They had 2
children:

11. Sarah Churchill	b. February 18, 1969	d.
11. Hannah Bigelow	b. November 5, 1971	d.

John & Linda divorced on May 25, 1980.
John had 2 children by **Anne-Marie Barbara Aigner** (b. December 10, 1945 d.   ) daughter of
Lucien Lazlo & Mady Anne (Lenard) Aigner

11. Samantha Lenard	b. February 12, 1981	d.
11. Adam Scott	b. September 15, 1984	d.

John on July 11, 1992 married **Patricia Cheryl Pedlow** (b. December 25, 1947 d.   ) daughter of
Donald Ellis & Margaret Joan (Ford) Pedlow of Indianapolis, IN. She had 2 children in a past union.

11. Shalane Grace Flanagan	b. July 8, 1981	d.
11. Maggie Clare Flanagan	b. December 28, 1983	d.

10. **Lindsey Crawford Churchill, Jr** on July 7, 1957 married **Roberta Gail Lester** (b. September 29, 1933
d.   ) daughter of Leonard & Shirley (Siegel) Lester of Roslyn, NY. They had 2 children:

11. Dana Lester	b. January 5, 1961	d.
11. Lauren Sarah "Laurie"	b. September 18, 1964	d.

10. **John Preston Churchill** on August 19, 1967 married **Faith Anne Scalise** (b. April 13, 1941 d.   )
    daughter of James Joseph & Adeline Lillian (Marinelli) Scalise of New Britain, CT. They had 2 children:

11. Anne Elizabeth	b. February 25, 1969	d.
11. Alison Jane	b. April 7, 1972	d.

10. **Merton Eugene Gentleman Jr** on May 2, 1954 married **Charlotte Louise Maynard** (b. March 26, 1926
    d. November 12, 2009) daughter of Reed Lewis & Anna (Cubbinson) Maynard of Beloit, KS. They had
    2 children:

11. Duane Eugene	b. February 2, 1956	d.
11. Lynn Olin	b. October 11, 1958	d.

10. **Lawrence B Gentleman** on March 21, 1954 married **Betty Lou Thiessen** (b. December 2, 1934 d.   )
    daughter of Ernest C & Anna (Schmeil) Thiessen of Beloit, KS. They had 2 children:

11. Sharon Kay	b. October 5, 1956	d.
11. Kathryn Jo	b. June 11, 1960	d.

10. **Shirley Jeanne Libby** on June 11, 1946 married **John Bunyan Smith, Jr** (b. January 9, 1916 d. April
    2, 1981) son of John Bunyan Sr & Mary (Lilly) Smith of Jacksonville, FL. They had 2 children:

11. Carolyn Sue	b. September 21, 1948	d.
11. Sharon Ann	b. September 18, 1951	d.

Shirley on July 26, 1984 married **Frank G Love** (b. October 7, 1922 d.   ) son of John & Eola Love
of Lafayette, LA. Shirley & Frank had no children.

10. **Carolyn Lou Libby** on October 18, 1949 married **Edwin Lamar Dennis Jr** (b. June 29, 1926 d. August
    27, 2012) son of Edwin Lamar Sr & Maurice (Gormandy) Dennis of Baton Rouge, LA. They had 2
    children:

11. Adele Lynn	b. January 11, 1954	d.
11. Laura Leigh	b. February 1, 1955	d.

11. **Ruth Moran** on June 14, 1967 married **James Alan Wilson** (b. November 25, 1946 d.   ) son of
    Fred & Dorothy (Payne) Wilson of Tucson, AZ. They had 3 children:

12. Christina	b. July 24, 1968	d.
12. Cindy Kay	b. August 14, 1971	d.
12. Raymond Elliot	b. May 31, 1978	d.

11. **Thomas Olin Moran** on June 23, 1982 married **Helga Spradley** (b. November 24, 1931 d.   )
    daughter of Fritz & Hedwig Fuechsel of Gera, Germany. Thomas & Helga had no children.

11. **Julie Moran** on August 21, 1971 married **Lonnie M Bagwell** (b. August 16, 1951 d.   ) son of
    Andrew Jackson & Blanche Bagwell of Nashville TN. They had 2 children:

12. Julie Renee	b. December 12, 1974	d.
12. Andrew Clinton	b. January 20, 1978	d.

11. **Claire Moran**

11. **Marshall Wendall Weeks**

11. **Emily Susan Weeks** on May 19, 1979 married **Michael Lee Cox** (b. October 6, 1952 d.   ) son of Ralph & Leona Cox of W Buxton, ME. They had 1 child:

    12. Katherine Leslie   b. July 12, 1981   d.

Emily & Michael divorced on July 12, 1985.

11. **Susan Beth Churchill** on October 22, 1988 married **Thomas Schmidt** (b. February 4, 1963 d.   ) son of Henry & Lorraine Schmidt of San Diego, CA.

Susan & Thomas had no children & divorced on October 12, 1990.

Susan on June 8, 2002 married **Martin Richard Moran** (b. October 17. 1961 d.   ) son of Martin Ernest & Nancy Christine (Sansone) Moran of S Harwich, MA. Susan & Martin had no children.

11. **Steven Mark Churchill** on May 21, 1988 married **Dawn Frankel** (b. November 8, 1963 d.   ) daughter of George & Gertrude (Hagelin) Frankel of New York, NY. They had 1 child:

    12. Spencer Charles   b. September 30, 1991   d.

11. **Lynn Donna Churchill** on June 12, 1976 married **Steven Coates** (b. September 24, 1953 d.   ) son of Bruce & Coleen (Richardson) Coates of Kezar Falls, ME. They had 1 child:

    12. Jason Steven   b. January 20, 1985   d.

Lynn & Steven divorced in June 1988.

Lynn on June 18, 1988 married **Richard Edward Seamans** (b. October 6, 1943 d.   ) son of Wilmer E & Marion S (Kirker) Seamans of Kezar Falls, ME. They had 1 child:

    12. Eric Joseph   b. December 7, 1990   d.

11. **Dawn Linda Churchill** on June 12, 1976 married **Tim Stocks** (b. July 23, 1954 d.   ) son of Donald & Dorothy (Doe) Stocks of S Hiram, ME. They had 2 children:

    12. Jeffrey Allen   b. August 28, 1978   d.

    12. Christopher   b. August 17, 1980   d.

11. **Robert Alan Churchill** on February 27, 1982 married **Patricia Garland Higgens** "Tuney" (b. March 24, 1951 d.   ) daughter of John & Jane (Phillips) Garland of Salem, MA. They had 1 child:

    12. Cass Randolph   b. November 11, 1986   d.

Robert & Patricia divorced in 1999.

Robert on March 20, 2004 married **Holly Ann Compare** (b. June 9, 1961 d.   ) daughter of Don Paul & Marsha Ann (Reid) Soloer of East Boothby, ME..Robert & Holly had no children. Holly had 1 child in a previous union:

    12. Hailey Paige   b. February 10, 1990   d.

11. **Cheryl Lee Black** on May 25, 1985 married **Wayne Christopher Ives** (b. March 22, 1961 d.   ) son of Rev A Christopher & Marilyn (Macomber) Ives of Londonderry, NH. They had 3 children:

    12. Alexis Catherine Jade   b. April 20, 1987   d.

    12. Stuart Nicholas Henry   b. December 12, 1989   d.

    12. Eric Samuel David   b. September 19, 1994   d.

11. **James Fredrick Black** on September 19, 1998 married **Jennifer Lillian Crommet** (b. April 14, 1971 d.   ) daughter of Larry Milton & Carole (Wambolt) Crommet of Portland, Me. They had 2 children:

    12. Alexandra Leigh   b. December 7, 2001   d.

    12. Carson James   b. November 2, 2004   d.

11. **John Carroll Black** on November 21, 2007 married **Meredith Lynn Bliss** (b. March 18, 1969 d.   ) daughter of Leighton Roy & Karen L (Goldthwaite) Bliss of W Baldwin, ME.

11. **Lorie Lee Pike** on August 8, 1981 married **Robert William Sturgeon** (b. August 30, 1954 d.   ) son of William Luwellyn & Theresa (Day) Sturgeon of Cornish, ME. They had 2 children:

    12. Michael David   b. April 3, 1984   d.

    12. Andrea Lynn   b. December 30, 1985   d.

Lorie & Robert divorced in 1997.

Lorie on October 3, 1999 married **Rodney Lee Gilpatrick** (b. October 20, 1956 d. October 30, 2015) son of Erland LeRoy & Maude Sue Woodman Gilpatrick of Parsonsfield, ME. Lorie & Rodney had no children.

11. **David Wyer Pike** on June 21, 1986 married **Denise Livernois** (b. March 4, 1953 d.   ) daughter of Leon & Mary (LeBoutillier) Livernois of Southbridge, MA. They had 2 children:

    12. Chad Robert   b. February 4, 1987   d.

    12. Katherine Lee   b. February 13, 1988   d.

11. **Elizabeth Godfrey Tucker** on May 20, 1984 married **Dr. Geoffrey David Gould** (b. October 11, 1939 d.   ) son of David Winfield & Grace (Hendrickson) Gould of Minneapolis, MN. They had 1 child:

    12. Peter Coryell   b. April 25, 1985   d.

11. **Sarah Lowell Tucker** on August 28, 1989 married **David John Owens** (b. February 1, 1941 d.   ) son of David C & Iona (Pomeroy) Owens of Utica, NY. Sarah & David had no children & divorced in 2001.

11. **Margaret Sayre Tucker** on June 23, 1978 married **William Charles Mitchell, Jr** (b. September 7, 1952 d.   ) son of William Charles Sr. & Helen (Yates) Mitchell of Louisville, KY. They had 3 children:

    12. Andrew Russell   b. February 7, 1983   d.

    12. Susan Anne   b. September 18, 1986   d.

    12. Brian Thomas   b. September 11, 1989   d.

11. **Susan Seabury Hays** on May 31, 1980 married **Daniel James Whalen** (b. June 9, 1949 d.   ) son of David James & Virginia Frances (Evers) Whalen of Tomahawk, WI. They had 2 children:

    12. James David   b. August 4, 1984   d.

    12. Thomas Hopkins   b. December 12, 1987   d.

11. **David Libby Hays** on February 13, 2005 married **Anna Roth** (b. February 26, 1959 d.   ) daughter of Henry & Sylvia Ellen (Grossberg) Roth of S. Nyack, NY. They had 2 children:

    12. Benjamin Maxwell   b. August 2, 2006   d.

    12. Will McGowen   b. August 2, 2006   d.

11. **Daniel McGowan Hays** on February 19, 1984 married **Ludmila Borisovna** (b. June 7, 1956 d.   ) daughter of Boris Alexendrovich & Nina Nikolaevna (Ukhova) Borisovna of Leningrad, USSR. Daniel & Ludmila had no children & divorced in November 1991.

11. **Nancy Carol Lord**

11. **Susan Diane Lord** on August 30, 1969 married **David Alan Dixon** (b. August 18, 1940 d. September 2, 1982) son of Ralph Edwin & Ruth (Conley) Dixon of Battle Creek, MI. They had 3 children:

    12. Diane Lynne   b. December 19, 1971   d.

    12. Aimee Leigh   b. March 14, 1975   d.

    12. Audre Ruth   b. October 14, 1981   d.

11. **Donna Jeanne Lord** on July 4, 1993 married **Joseph Hussey Kendall** (b. June 11, 1949 d.   ) son of Leon Ellsworth & Barbara May (Hussey) Kendall of Cornish, ME. He had 2 children in a previous union

    12. Ryan Joseph   b. October 12, 1983   d.

    12. Angela Mae   b. October 6, 1986   d.

Donna Jeanne & Joseph had no children.

11. **Geoffrey Stacy Lord** on November 27, 1968 married **Janet Irene Jepson** (b. September 21, 1950 d.   ) daughter of Oscar Lester & Elaine (Parker) Jepson of Berwick, ME. Geoff & Janet had no children & divorced in June 1980.
Geoff on August 23, 1980 married **Ellen Douglas McCausland** (b. September 4, 1959 d.   ) daughter of Thomas & Jean (Black) McCausland of Monkton, MD. Geoff & Ellen had no children.

11. **Joseph Merrill Lord** on October 4, 1975 married **Susan Holly Ripley** (b. December 23, 1952 d. daughter of Claire Edward & Beverly Madeline (Weeks) Ripley of Sheepscot, ME. They had 1 child:

    12. Josieda Marie "Sadie"   b. February 6, 1982   d.

J Merrill & Susan divorced in October 1991.
J Merrill on August 1, 1992 married **Candace Rogers** (b. April 18, 1960 d.   ) daughter of Theodore Alan & Jane (Allen) Rogers of Port Townsend, WA. They had 1 child:

    12. Calvin Ambrose   b. December 9, 1993   d.

J Merrill & Candace divorced in 1997
J Merrill on March 28, 1998 married **Shelley Gravino** (b. September 27, 1959 d.   ) daughter of Guido Dominec & Evelyn Ruth (Giardina) Gravino of Niagara Falls, NY. J Merrill & Shelley had no children.

11. **Robyn Jeanne Lord** on September 30, 1989 married **Richard Allen Austin** (b. August 16, 1956 d.   ) son of Richard Henry & Carol Jane (White) Austin of Nashua, NH. They had 2 children:

    12. Molly Lord   b. December 18, 1991   d.

    12. Max Philip   b. January 19, 1994   d.

Robyn & Richard divorced in 2001.

Robyn on February 25, 2007 married **Paul Allen Nichols** (b. July 27, 1966 d.   ) son of George Allen & Martha Ann (Martin) Nichols of Rome, GA. Robyn & Paul had no children.

11. **Dana Wadleigh Lord** on December 11, 1993 married **Shirley Dagmar Zeisberg** (b. January 19, 1950 d.   ) from Germany. Dana & Shirley had no children.

11. **Alan David Lord** on December 29, 1990 married **Anne Clemens Hendershott** (b. July 8, 1959 d.   ) daughter of Charles & Jacquelynn (Vizzini) Hendershott of New Orleans, LA.
Alan & Anne had no children & divorced on February 3, 1994.
Alan on December 17, 1994 married **Margaret Knott** "Margi" (b. October 6, 1959 d.   ) daughter of Sydney Tucker Jr & Ruth Ellen (Senate) Knott of Barnstable, MA. Alan & Margaret had no children.

11. **Leigh Ann Bonney** on September 9, 2000 married **Larry Ritzhaupt** (b. March 10, 1949 d.   ) son of Delbert Samuel & Iva Louise (Britton) Ritzhaupt of Galion, OH. Leigh & Larry had no children.

11. **Jonathan Daniel Lord** on August 6, 1988 married **Jill Marie Christofferson** (b. April 1, 1955 d.   ) daughter of Robert Stanley & Grace Irene (Smith) Christofferson of Hibbing, MN. They had 1 child:

    12. Jonathan Daniel Jr. "Daniel" │ b. March 6, 1989   │ d.

11. **Jay Merrill Lord II** on October 27, 1990 married **Priscilla Ann Sawyer** (b. March 14, 1962 d.   ) daughter of Jeremy Jason & Barbara (Harmon) Sawyer of Hampton, NH. They had 1 child:

    12. Calvin Merrill   b. December 22, 1992   d.

11. **David Kimball Lord**

11. **Nathan Andrew Fates** on June 10, 2000 married **Corey Patricia Pike** (b. January 19, 1973 d.   ) daughter of Kenneth Thorton & Paula Marie (Powers) Pike of South Portland, ME. They had 1 child:

    12. Sophia Sage   b. December 21, 2005   d.

Nathan & Corey divorced on December 8, 2017.

11. **Justin Joshua Faatz** on August 27, 2005 married **Sarah Rosalind Rogers** (b. May 31, 1975 d. daughter of Scott Guy & Vicki Ray (Porter) Rogers of Unity, ME. They had 2 children:

    12. Joshua Nicholas   b. April 22, 2007   d.

    12. Anna Elizabeth   b. May 25, 2010   d.

11. **Robyn Dayle Pettengill** on September 25, 2004 married **Dana Violette** (b. November 6, 1965 d.   ) son of Marcel Sr. & Roberta Jean (Paulsen) Violette, of Cumberland, ME Robyn & Dana had no children & divorced on August 16, 2017.

11. **Jennifer Lord Pettengill** on October 5, 1996 married **Jay Kenneth Banks** (b. August 5, 1964 d.   )
son of Harland William & Betty Lou (Dodge) Banks of Gorham, ME. They had 4 children:

12. Jackson Audway	b. June 1, 1999	d.
12. Georgia Elizabeth	b. January 12, 2001	d.
12. Griffin William	b. November 27, 2002	d.
12. Jay Hudson	b. April 24, 2008	d.

Jennifer & Jay divorced January 2, 2014.

11. **Sarah Churchill Treworgy** on June 29, 2002 married **John de LaChapelle** (b. October 15, 1961
d.   ) son of Richard Passerat & Patricia Ruth (Fisher) de LaChapelle of Oak Harbor, WA. They
had 2 children:

12. Finn Stuart	b September 9, 2005	d.
12. Jack Edward	b. July 31, 2008	d.

11. **Hannah Bigelow Treworgy** on February 28, 2005 married **George Ekwere** (b. May 25, 1976 d.   )
son of Joseph Ekwere & Magrete Luma of Limbe, South West Province, Cameroon. They had 1 child:

12. Jasper Bigelow	b. June 24, 2009	d.

Hannah & George divorced November 4, 2016.

11. **Samantha Lenard Aigner-Treworgy**

11. **Adam Scott Aigner-Treworgy** on September 5, 2015 married **Susan Joyce Davis** (b. November 10,
1979 d.   ) daughter of Gerald Vincent & Anne Veronica (Torpey) Davis of Philadelphia, PA.

11. **Dana Lester Churchill** on July 6, 2003 married **Wei Wang** (b. July 23, 1962 d.   ) daughter of
Yongfu & Yunzhi (Zhou) Wang of Dandong, Liaoning, China. Wei had a child in a previous union.

12. Wayne Zhang	b. March 16, 1986	d.

Dana & Wei had no children.

11. **Lauren Sarah Churchill**

11. **Anne Elizabeth Churchill**

11. **Alison Jane Churchill** on July 14, 2007 married **Michael Klezos** (b. March 1, 1971 d. July 7, 2010) son
of Stanley & Linda Grace (Wood) Klezos of W. Hartford, CT. Allison & Michael had no children.

11. **Duane Eugene Gentleman** on July 16, 1978 married **Cheryl D Powell** (b. June 12, 1956 d.   )
daughter of Donald & Bonnie Powell of Ottowa, KS. They had 2 children:

12. Sarah Diane	b. March 8, 1985	d.
12. Nathan Eugene	b. March 22, 1992	d.

11. **Lynn Olin Gentleman**

11. **Sharon Kay Gentleman** on July 19, 1975 married **James David Kindscher** (b. November 7, 1955 d.   ) son of John Jacob & Doris James Kindscher of Beloit, KS. They had 2 children:

12. Lauren Raissa	b. April 16, 1981	d.
12. Allison Kay	b. February 11, 1984	d.

Sharon & James divorced in 1984.
Sharon on September 13, 1993 married **John C Fuller** (b. September 10, 1945 d.   ) son of Ansell C. & Polly Spain Fuller of Beloit, KS. Sharon & John had no children.

11. **Kathryn Jo Gentleman** on July 18, 1981 married **David Bruce Grabbe** (b. March 3, 1956 d.   ) son of Clarence & Lillian Grabbe of Hays, KS. They had 2 children:

12. Cody Taylor	b. November 17, 1985	d.
12. Kaylee Brynn	b. May 24, 1988	d.

11. **Carolyn Sue Smith** on April 20, 1974 married **Martin Anthony Petrich III** (b. December 21, 1942 d.   ) son of Martin Jr & Jean Clark Petrich of Lafayette, LA. They had 2 children:

12. Benjamin Clark	b. April 6, 1977	d.
12. Ian Norris	b. October 29, 1980	d.

11. **Sharon Ann Smith** on November 22, 1979 married **Curley James Darby** (b. December 9, 1948 d.   ) son of Leroy & Emily Darby of Lafayette, LA. They had 2 children:

12. Luke William	b. December 1, 1986	d.
12. Kelly Carolyn	b. February 6, 1990	d.

11. **Adele Lynne Dennis** on August 7, 1976 married **David Patrick White** (b. December 13, 1952 d.   ) son of Patrick William & Mary Jones White of Virginia Beach, VA. They had 2 children:

12. Christopher David	b. September 2, 1984	d.
12. Courtney Lynn Adele	b. December 9, 1986	d.

11. **Laura Leigh Dennis** on December 29, 1982 married **Jack Moulton Schmidt** (b. February 1, 1955 d.   ) son of Jack & Gladys Schmidt of Virginia Beach, VA. They had 2 children:

12. Jennifer Libby	b. August 25, 1985	d.
12. Jessica Ingrid	b. July 25, 1989	d.

12. **Christina Wilson**

12. **Cindy Kay Wilson** on July 17, 1993 married **Michael Dalton Curtis** (b. June 1, 1973 d.   ) son of Gary Dalton & Janet Ely Curtis of Safford, AZ. They had 1 child:

13. Makaila Rayne	b. January 7, 1994	d.

12. **Raymond Elliot Wilson**

12. **Julie Renee Bagwell**

12. **Andrew Clinton Bagwell**

12. **Katherine Leslie Cox**

12. **Spencer Charles Churchill**

12. **Jason Steven Coates**

12. **Eric Joseph Seamans**

12. **Jeffrey Allen Stocks** on July 7, 2001 married **Rebecca Joy McNeil** (b. August 21, 1978 d.   )
daughter of Gary Wayne & Brenda Louise (Howe) McNeil of Baldwin, ME. They had 2 children:

13. Isaac Timothy	b. June 4, 2002	d.
13. Caleb Andrew	b. February 21, 2005	d.

Jeff & Rebecca divorced in 2007.

12. **Christopher Stocks** had 2 children with **Michelle Perkins** (b. August 21, 1978 d.   ) daughter of
Westley Thomas & Cynthia Rosa (Shaw) Perkins of Portland, ME.

13. Olivia Rosana	b. April 16, 1997	d.
13. Dylan Christopher	b. September 6, 2004	d.

12. **Cass Randolph Churchill** had 1 child with **Elizabeth Pierie** (b. November 7, 1986 d.   ) daughter
of Lawrence & Jodie (Thiriault) Pierie of Portland, ME.

13. Emma Jean	b. September 14, 2012

12. **Alexis Catherine Jade Ives**

12. **Stuart Nicholas Henry Ives**

12. **Eric Samuel David Ives**

12. **Alexandra Leigh Black**

12. **Carson James Black**

12. **Michael David Sturgeon** on September 1, 2012 married **Heidi Sinclair Morrill** (b. June 27, 1985
d.   ) daughter of Dan Andrew & Laurie Ann (Crommet) Morrill of Cornish, ME. They had 1 child:

13. Reese Caroline	b. September 23. 2014	d.
13 Maci Jane	b. January 19, 2018	d.

12. **Andrea Lynn Sturgeon** on September 20, 2014 married **Joshua Brian Emmons** (b. February 22, 1985
d.   ) son of Terry G & Celeste Ann (Beleckis) Emmons of Denmark, ME They had 1 child:

13. Daniel Robert	b. October 29. 2015	d.

12. **Chad Robert Pike** on August 20, 2016 married **Renee Sarah Daigle** (b. January 29, 1986 d.   )
daughter of Richard Aurel & Joan (Cumberland) Daigle of Madawaska, ME.

12. **Katherine Lee Pike**

12. **Peter Coryell Gould** on July 20, 2018 married **Elizabeth Anne Francis** (b. December 29, 1991 d.   ) daughter of John Leroy & Kelley (Sax) Francis of Johnson City, NH.

12. **Andrew Russell Mitchell** on April 17, 2013 married **Rebecca Catherine Riggs** (b. February 16, 1990 d.   ) daughter of Christopher Thomas & Glenda Rachel Hill (Evers) Riggs of Westcliffe, CO. They had 2 children:

13. Jack William	b. September 1, 2013	d.
13. Grace Tucker	b. June 28, 2016	d.

12. **Susan Anne Mitchell** on July 14, 2009 married **Matthew Joseph Miller** (b. January 4, 1987 d.   ) son of Mark Miller & Molly (Tate) Matheny of Nashville, TN. They had 1 child:

13. Lilly Anne	b. December 17, 2009	d.

12. **Brian Thomas Mitchell** on May 28, 2016 married **Lindsey Tenneson** (b. August 21, 1990 d.   ) daughter of

12. **James David Whalen**

12. **Thomas Hopkins Whalen** on August 8, 2014 married **Abby Louise Blinkhorn** (b. August 28, 1983 d.   ) daughter of William & Marilyn (Helena) Blinkhorn of Portland, ME.

12. **Benjamin Maxwell Hays**

12. **Will McGowan Hays**

12. **Diane Lynne Dixon** on July 10, 1999 married **Donald Wesley Underwood** (b. November 10, 1971 d.   ) son of Donald Lloyd & Carolyn (Caldwell) Underwood of Gobles, MI. They had 2 children:

13. Gibson David	b. May 14, 2001	d.
13. Baxter Donald	b. July 22, 2006	d. July 22, 2006

12. **Aimee Leigh Dixon** had 1 child by **Ronald Dean Burgess** son of Ronald Elbert & Pauline Elizabeth (Lynch) Burgess of Nederland, CO.

13. Sadira Nadine Burgess	b. August 7, 2000	d.

Aimee on September 18, 2010 married **Randall Mark Staples** (b. July 2, 1959 d.   ) son of Mark Paul & Jeaneen Atlantis (Senjem) Staples of Star Prairie, WI. Aimee & Randall had no children.

12. **Audre Ruth Dixon** on August 8, 2017 married **Ronald Raymond Rabb Jr** (b. May 4, 1981 d.   ) son of Ronald Raymond Sr & Suzanne Pearl (Moser) Rabb of Kalamazoo, MI. They had 2 children:

13. Lucius Raymond	b. December 4, 2011	d.
13. Wyleigh Jay	b. September 20, 2013	d.

12. **Josieda Marie Lord** on July 7, 2018 married **Kyle Robert Pettit** (b. October 7, 1984 d.   ) son of Donald Richard & Jo Ann (Parker) Pettit of Santa Rosa, CA.

12. **Calvin Ambrose Lord**

12. **Molly Lord Austin**

12. **Max Phillip Austin**

12. **Jonathan Daniel Lord, Jr**

12. **Calvin Merrill Lord**

12. **Sophia Sage Fates**

12. **Joshua Nicholas Faatz**

12. **Anna Elizabeth Faatz**

12. **Jackson Audway Banks**

12. **Georgia Elizabeth Banks**

12. **Griffin William Banks**

12. **Jay Hudson Banks**

12. **Finn Stuart de LaChapelle**

12. **Jack Edward de LaChapelle**

12. **Jasper Bigelow Ekwere**

12. **Sarah Diane Gentleman**

12. **Nathan Eugene Gentleman**

12. **Lauren Raissa Kindscher**

12. **Allison Kay Kindscher**

12. **Cody Taylor Grabbe**

12. **Kaylee Brynn Grabbe**

12. **Benjamin Clark Petrich**

12. **Ian Norris Petrich**

12. **Luke William Darby**

12. **Kelly Carolyn Darby**

12. **Christopher David White**

12. **Courtney Lynn Adele White**

12. **Jennifer Libby Schmidt**

12. **Jessica Ingrid Schmidt**

13. **Makaila Rayne Curtis**

13. **Isaac Timothy Stocks**

13. **Caleb Andrew Stocks**

13. **Olivia Rosana Stocks**

13. **Dylan Christopher Stocks**

13. **Emma Jean Churchill**

13. **Reese Caroline Sturgeon**

13. **Maci Jane Sturgeon**

13. **Daniel Robert Emmons**

13. **Jack William Mitchell**

13. **Grace Tucker Mitchell**

13. **Lilly Anne Miller**

13. **Gibson David Underwood**

13. **Baxter Donald Underwood** never married or had children

13. **Sadira Nadine Burgess**

13. **Lucius Raymond Rabb**

13. **Wyleigh Jay Rabb**

DESCENDANTS OF
THOMAS SMITH CHURCHILL, JR &
MARY ANN DIXON

7. **Thomas Smith Churchill, Jr** on January 1, 1855 married **Mary Ann Dixon** (b. October 2, 1832 d. December 30, 1878) daughter of William Dennett & Mary Dearborn Dixon of N Parsonsfield, ME. They had 3 children:

8. Eva	b. November 19, 1856	d. September 13, 1883
8. William Dennett Dixon	b. October 6, 1858	d. January 19, 1940
8. Thomas G	b. November 20, 1863	d. November 13, 1878

Thomas Jr in March 14, 1882 married **Olive Bowers Roberts** of Whitestown, NY. Thomas & Olive had no children.

8. **Eva Churchill** in June 1, 1876 married **Joseph Boothby** (b. August 11, 1854 d. October 29, 1919) son of Samuel & Rebecca (Moulton) Boothby of Parsonsfield, ME. They had 1 child:

9. Lillian R "Birdie"	b. September 15, 1878	d. June 23, 1916

After Eva's death Joseph married again and moved to FL.

8. **William Dennet Dixon Churchill** on December 22, 1880 married **Clara Mabel Sweat** (b. September 14, 1859 d. April 12, 1900) daughter of Dr. Moses E & Rebecca Sweat of N Parsonsfield, ME. They had 1 child:

9. Harry William	b. December 29, 1884	d. November 16, 1937

8. **Thomas G Churchill** never married or had children.

9. **Lillian R Boothby** on December 12, 1897 married **Edgar Porter Jackson** (b. June 7, 1876 d. August 1, 1964) They had 1 child:

10. Lucille	b. 1899	d.

9. **Harry William Churchill** on November 20, 1910 married **Edna Anise Anderson** (b. March 19, 1886 d. November 7, 1972) daughter of William H & Annie (Morris) Anderson of Brooklyn, NY. They had 3 children:

10. Thomas William	b. June 27, 1913	d. December 8, 1979
10. Mabel Harriet	b. October 7, 1915	d. May 20, 2009
10. Ruth Louise	b. February 17, 1920	d.

10. **Lucille Jackson** never married or had children.

10. **Thomas William Churchill** never married or had children.

10. **Mabel Harriet Churchill** on October 25, 1947 married **Jesse Clinton Moran** (b. March 5, 1914 d. July 15, 1961) son of J Homer & Ada (Fuller) Moran of Manchester, GA. They had 4 children:

11. Ruth	b. October 14, 1948	d.
11. Thomas Olin	b. September 11, 1949	d. February 23, 1984
11. Julie	b. December 3, 1950	d.
11. Claire	b. March 27, 1952	d.

10. **Ruth Louise Churchill** on November 23, 1946 married **George Walter Weeks** (b. March 5, 1919 d. September 28, 1951) son of Howard E & Florence (Thornton) Weeks of E Parsonsfield, ME. They had 2 children:

11. Marshall Wendell	b. August 7, 1947	d.
11. Emily Susan	b. April 22, 1950	d.

Ruth on July 16, 1973 married **David Lester Jewell** (b. January 25, 1914 d.   ) son of John J & Emma Mae Jewell of Kezar Falls, ME. Ruth & David had no children.

11. **Ruth Moran** on June 14, 1967 married **James Alan Wilson** (b. November 25, 1946 d.   ) son of Fred & Dorothy (Payne) Wilson of Tucson, AZ. They had 3 children:

12. Christina	b. July 24, 1968	d.
12. Cindy Kay	b. August 14, 1971	d.
12. Raymond Elliot	b. May 31, 1978	d.

11. **Thomas Olin Moran** on June 23, 1982 married **Helga Spradley** (b. November 24, 1931 d.   ) daughter of Fritz & Hedwig Fuechsel of Gera, Germany. Thomas & Helga had no children.

11. **Julie Moran** on August 21, 1971 married **Lonnie M Bagwell** (b. August 16, 1951 d.   ) son of Andrew Jackson & Blanche Bagwell of Nashville, TN. They had 2 children:

12. Julie Renee	b. December 12, 1974	d.
12. Andrew Clinton	b. January 20, 1978	d.

11. **Claire Moran**

11. **Marshall Wendall Weeks**

11. **Emily Susan Weeks** on May 19, 1979 married **Michael Lee Cox** (b. October 6, 1952 d.   ) son of Ralph & Leona Cox of W Buxton, ME. They had 1 child:

12. Katherine Leslie	b. July 12, 1981	d.

Emily & Michael divorced on July 12, 1985.

12. **Christina Wilson**

12. **Cindy Kay Wilson** on July 17, 1993 married **Michael Dalton Curtis** (b. June 1, 1973 d.   ) son of Gary Dalton & Janet Ely Curtis of Safford, AZ. They had 1 child:

13. Makaila Rayne	b. January 7, 1994	d.

12. **<u>Raymond Elliot Wilson</u>**

12. **<u>Julie Renee Bagwell</u>**

12. **<u>Andrew Clinton Bagwell</u>**

12. **<u>Katherine Leslie Cox</u>**

13. **<u>Makaila Rayne Curtis</u>**

DESCENDANTS OF OTIS BANKS CHURCHILL & SUSAN E FERREN

7. **Otis Banks Churchill** on January 2, 1861 married **Susan E Ferren** (b. January 14, 1839 d. January 7, 1911) daughter of James & Sally (Woodman) Ferren of Freedom, NH. They had 3 children:

8. Wilbur F	b. April 24, 1862	d. June 19, 1862
8. Charles Clarence	b. June 2, 1863	d. May 18, 1905
8. Sarah May	b. June 8, 1865	d. December 20, 1934

8. **Wilbur F Churchill** never married or had children.

8. **Charles Clarence Churchill** on February 14, 1891 married **Ida Belle Chapman** (b. July 5, 1869 d. June 13, 1952) daughter of George Frank & Mary (Hussey) Chapman of N Parsonsfield, ME. They had 2 children:

9. Lord Randolph	b. February 4, 1899	d. December 2, 1975
9. Helen May	b. May 24, 1902	d. December 14, 1996

8. **Sarah May Churchill** on August 30, 1893 married **Joseph Merrill Lord** (b. October 29, 1865 d. February 27, 1920) son of Daniel & Josephine Burbank (Merrill) Lord of N Parsonsfield, ME. They had 5 children:

9. Theresa Churchill	b. November 27, 1894	d. June 26, 1969
9. Frank Wadleigh	b. January 3, 1897	d. February 21, 1979
9. Myron Otis	b. January 19, 1899	d. July 17, 1951
9. Daniel Bertram	b. September 18, 1901	d. September 25, 1959
9. Phyllis Evelyn	b. May 27, 1909	d. December 30, 2002

9. **Lord Randolph Churchill** on October 16, 1926 married **Marguerite Grace Marston** (b. December 6, 1905 d. January 7, 1996) daughter of Dr. Clarence & Lula (Richardson) Marston of Brownfield, ME. They had 2 children:

10. Charles Clarence II	b. September 7, 1927	d. April 10, 2016
10. Robert Winston	b. June 12, 1930	d. May 4, 2008

9. **Helen May Churchill** on June 26, 1929 married **Verne McAllister Black** (b. July 19, 1902 d. August 5, 1988) son of Orion & Mabel (McAllister) Black of Kezar Falls, ME. They had 2 children:

10. James Orion	b. November 10, 1930	d. October 17, 2005
10. Laura Jane	b. August 23, 1932	d. February 24, 2017

9. **Theresa Churchill Lord** on January 22, 1921 married **Donald Maxwell Libby** (b. September 26, 1896 d. March 29, 1972) son of Frank Willard & Elizabeth (Philpot) Libby of Limerick, ME. They had 2 children:

10. Kathryn Churchill	b. May 27, 1922	d. December 1, 1994
10. Joanne Elizabeth "Jose"	b. August 13, 1926	d.

9. **Frank Wadleigh Lord** on September 17, 1919 married **Ruth Doris Verbeck** (b. January 1, 1895 d. January 20, 1980) daughter of Calvin & Ida (Hadlock) Verbeck of Malden, MA. They had 3 children:

10. Jay Merrill	b. July 28, 1921	d. August 13, 1987
10. Howard Verbeck	b. March 8, 1924	d. August 8, 2013
10. Philip Wadleigh	b. February 4, 1926	d.

9. **Myron Otis Lord** on August 9, 1924 married **Edith Josephine Sweeney** "Jo" (b. January 25, 1899 d. April 28, 1975) daughter of Timothy & Eliza Jane (Gilliam) Sweeney of W Point, ME. Myron & Edith had no children.

9. **Daniel Bertram Lord** on December 26, 1930 married **Irene Stanley** (b. November 26, 1909 d. October 6, 1986) daughter of Everett George & Elma (Tarbox) Stanley of Kezar Falls, ME. They had 2 children:

10. Ann	b. September 20, 1931	d. February 13, 2005
10. David Merrill	b. December 16, 1936	d.

9. **Phyllis Evelyn Lord** on July 2, 1936 married **Audway Stuart Treworgy** "Stubby" (b. March 30, 1907 d. February 28, 1999) son of Paul Wilfred & Edith Sophia (Newcomb) Treworgy of Augusta, ME. They had 3 children:

10. Linda	b. November 23, 1942	d.
10. Martha	b. May 5, 1944	d. February 26, 2013
10. John Stuart	b. May 26, 1947	d.

10. **Charles Clarence Churchill II** on May 29, 1954 married **Nancy Ruth Dopp** (b. November 28, 1932 d.   ) daughter of Clarence Henry & Dorothy (Jenner) Dopp of Johnstown, NY. They had 2 children:

11. Susan Beth	b. July 15, 1958	d.
11. Steven Mark	b. April 26, 1960	d.

Charles & Nancy divorced in December 1969.
Charles on June 20, 1971 married **Nancy Jopp** (b. June 2, 1932 d. March 31, 2004) daughter of Kenneth & Evelyn Jopp of Delmar, NY. Charles & Nancy had no children & divorced on January 6, 1995.
Charles on August 18, 2013 married **Willa-Jo Mauger** (b. January 1, 1937 d.   ) daughter of Joseph Edward & Maxie Emma (Hopkins) Barricklow of Dabney, IN. Charles & Willa-Jo had no children.

10. **Robert Winston Churchill** on April 24, 1954 married **Dorothy Mae Leonard** (b. May 17, 1932 d.   ) daughter of Joseph Alfred & Susan (Moores) Leonard of Old Town, ME. They had 3 children:

11. Lynn Donna	b. July 1, 1955	d.
11. Dawn Linda	b. July 1, 1955	d.
11. Robert Alan	b. November 21, 1958	d.

10. **James Orion Black** on September 24, 1955 married **Charlotte Edwards** (b. December 1, 1934 d. November 21, 2007) daughter of Carroll & Eleanor (Bowie) Edwards of W Baldwin, ME. They had 3 children:

11. Cheryl Lee	b. January 28, 1961	d.
11. James Frederick	b. November 20, 1963	d.
11. John Carroll	b. December 19, 1964	d.

10. **Laura Jane Black** on February 5, 1954 married **Robert LeRoy Pike** (b. June 21, 1931 d. October 10, 2008) son of Robert Smith & Viola (Libby) Pike of Cornish, ME. They had 2 children:

11. Lorie Lee	b. January 16, 1957	d.
11. David Wyer	b. March 10, 1960	d.

10. **Kathryn Churchill Libby** on August 23, 1947 married **Frank Hammond Tucker** (b. December 29, 1923 d. January 26, 2017) son of Frank Edmund & Evalyn V (Godfrey) Tucker of Wilmington, DE. They had 3 children:

11. Elizabeth Godfrey "Libby"	b. November 29, 1948	d.
11. Sarah Lowell	b. April 18, 1951	d.
11. Margaret Sayre	b. September 8, 1954	d.

10. **Joanne Elizabeth Libby** "Jose" on June 23, 1948 married **David Ware Hays** (b. August 1, 1926 d. June 1, 1969) son of James McFadden & Rena Victoria (Green) Hays of Cape Elizabeth, ME. They had 3 children:

11. Susan Seabury	b. September 26, 1956	d.
11. David Libby "Buzz"	b. August 22, 1958	d.
11. Daniel McGowan	b. September 20, 1961	d. June 28, 2007

Joanne on April 29, 1995 married **Rev Fred Ingraham Glover** (b. June 13, 1924 d. April 28, 1996) son of John W Sr & Edith (Ingraham) Glover of Bangor, ME. Joanne & Fred had no children.

10. **Jay Merrill Lord** on November 13, 1943 married **Barbara Jane Appleton "Bobbie"** (b. July 21, 1920 d. July 31, 1993) daughter of Nelson Winfield & Caroline Stella (Metzger) Appleton of Jenkintown, PA. They had 3 children:

11. Nancy Carol	b. September 10, 1944	d.
11. Susan Diane	b. April 24, 1950	d.
11. Donna Jeanne	b. September 13, 1955	d.

10. **Howard Verbeck Lord** on August 16, 1945 married **Marilyn Leatrice Stacy** (b. April 7, 1925 d.   ) daughter of Lawrence & Isabelle (Sawyer) Stacy of Kezar Falls, ME. They had 2 children:

11. Geoffrey Stacy "Geoff"	b. February 12, 1947	d.
11. Joseph Merrill "J Merrill"	b. April 26, 1949	d.

Howard & Marilyn divorced in May 1982.

Howard on October 19, 1982 married **Connie Elizabeth Rossborough** (b. October 19, 1948 d. December 18, 2014) daughter of Paris & Jane (Bryant) Rossborough of Biddeford, ME. Howard & Connie had no children & divorced in 1997.

10. **Philip Wadleigh Lord** on June 21, 1952 married **Mary Alberta Henderson** (b. November 8, 1929 d.   ) daughter of Roderick Raymond & Helen Dorothy "Dot" (Davis) Henderson of W Baldwin, ME. They had 3 children:

11. Robyn Jeanne	b. February 21, 1954	d.
11. Dana Wadleigh	b. April 4, 1956	d.
11. Alan David	b. November 4, 1958	d.

10. **Ann Lord** on September 17, 1955 married **James Hall Bonney, MD** (b. September 5, 1927 d. October 27, 1994) son of Albert & Esther (Hall) Bonney of Bath ME. They had 1 child:

11. Leigh Anne	b. July 15, 1958	d.

10. **David Merrill Lord** on June 20, 1959 married **Martha Ann Dodge** (b. March 28, 1937 d.   ) daughter of John Sinclair & Miriam Lucy (Wentworth) Dodge of Brentwood, NH. They had 3 children:

11. Jonathan Daniel "Jon"	b. July 4, 1960	d.
11. Jay Merrill II	b. October 19, 1963	d.
11. David Kimball "Kim"	b. April 20, 1965	d.

David & Martha divorced on February 23, 1984.

10. **Linda Treworgy** on August 24, 1968 married **Wright Everett Faatz** (b. March 4, 1943 d.   ) son of Dr. Gerald Almon & Avis Josephine (Williams) Faatz of Unity, ME. They had 2 children:

11. Nathan Andrew	b. December 26, 1971	d.
11. Justin Joshua	b. January 20, 1976	d.

Linda & Wright divorced on June 16, 1979.

10. **Martha Treworgy** on August 5, 1967 married **Eric Mark Pettengill** (b. April 24, 1940 d.   ) son of George Waldo & Esther (Quigg) Pettengill of Island Falls, ME. They had 2 children:

11. Robyn Dayle	b. January 8, 1968	d.
11. Jennifer Lord	b. October 28, 1969	d.

Martha & Eric divorced in March 1972.

Martha on June 24, 1979 married **Robert Hulbert Harris** (b. November 6, 1931 d. January 17, 2012) son of Reginald Hulbert & Alice Eugenia (Hupper) Harris of Portland, ME. Martha & Robert had no children & divorced on September 9, 1993.

10. **John Stuart Treworgy** on December 31, 1968 married **Linda Lou Roghaar** (b. September 11, 1947 d.   ) daughter of George Edward Sr & Florence (Bigelow) Roghaar of Arlington, MA. They had 2 children:

11. Sarah Churchill	b. February 18, 1969	d.
11. Hannah Bigelow	b. November 5, 1971	d.

John & Linda divorced on May 25, 1980.

John had 2 children by **Anne-Marie Barbara Aigner** (b. December 10, 1945 d.   ) daughter of Lucien Lazlo & Mady Anne (Lenard) Aigner

11. Samantha Lenard	b. February 12, 1981	d.
11. Adam Scott	b. September 15, 1984	d.

John on July 11, 1992 married **Patricia Cheryl Pedlow** (b. December 25, 1947 d.   ) daughter of Donald Ellis & Margaret Joan (Ford) Pedlow of Indianapolis, IN. She had 2 children in a past union.

| 11. Shalane Grace Flanagan | b. July 8, 1981 | d. |
| 11. Maggie Clare Flanagan | b. December 28, 1983 | d. |

11. **Susan Beth Churchill** on October 22, 1988 married **Thomas Schmidt** (b. February 4, 1963 d.   ) son of Henry & Lorraine Schmidt of San Diego, CA.
Susan & Thomas had no children & divorced on October 12, 1990.
Susan on June 8, 2002 married **Martin Richard Moran** (b. October 17. 1961 d.   ) son of Martin Ernest & Nancy Christine (Sansone) Moran of S Harwich, MA. Susan & Martin had no children.

11. **Steven Mark Churchill** on May 21, 1988 married **Dawn Frankel** (b. November 8, 1963 d.   ) daughter of George & Gertrude (Hagelin) Frankel of New York, NY. They had 1 child:

| 12. Spencer Charles | b. September 30, 1991 | d. |

11. **Lynn Donna Churchill** on June 12, 1976 married **Steven Coates** (b. September 24, 1953 d.   ) son of Bruce & Coleen Coates of Kezar Falls, ME. They had 1 child:

| 12. Jason Steven | b. January 10, 1985 | d. |

Lynn & Steven divorced in June 1988.
Lynn on June 18, 1988 married **Richard Edward Seamans** (b. October 6, 1943 d.   ) son of Wilmer E & Marion S (Kirker) Seamans of Kezar Falls, ME. They had 1 child:

| 12. Eric Joseph | b. December 7, 1990 | d. |

11. **Dawn Linda Churchill** on June 12, 1976 married **Tim Stocks** (b. July 23, 1954 d.   ) son of Donald & Dorothy (Doe) Stocks of S Hiram, ME. They had 2 children:

| 12. Jeffrey Allen | b. August 28, 1978 | d. |
| 12. Christopher | b. August 17, 1980 | d. |

11. **Robert Alan Churchill** on February 27, 1982 married **Patricia Garland Higgens** "Tuney" (b. March 24, 1951 d.   ) daughter of John & Jane (Phillips) Garland of Salem, MA. They had 1 child:

| 12. Cass Randolph | b. November 11, 1986 | d. |

Robert & Patricia divorced in 1999.
Robert on March 20, 2004 married **Holly Ann Compare** (b. June 9, 1961 d.   ) daughter of Don Paul & Marsha Ann (Reid) Soloer of East Boothby, ME. Robert & Holly had no children. Holly had 1 child in a previous union:

| 12. Hailey Paige | b. February 10, 1990 | d. |

11. **Cheryl Lee Black** on May 25, 1985 married **Wayne Christopher Ives** (b. March 22, 1961 d.   ) son of Rev A Christopher & Marilyn (Macomber) Ives of Londonderry, NH. They had 3 children:

12. Alexis Catherine Jade	b. April 20, 1987	d.
12. Stuart Nicholas Henry	b. December 12, 1989	d.
12. Eric Samuel David	b. September 19, 1994	d.

11. **James Fredrick Black** on September 19, 1998 married **Jennifer Lillian Crommet** (b. April 14, 1971 d.   ) daughter of Larry Milton & Carole (Wambolt) Crommet of Portland, ME. They had 2 children:

12. Alexandra Leigh	b. December 7, 2001	d.
12. Carson James	b. November 2, 2004	d.

11. **John Carroll Black** on November 21, 2007 married **Meredith Lynn Bliss** (b. March 18, 1969 d.   ) daughter of Leighton Roy Bliss & Karen L (Goldthwaite) of W Baldwin, ME.

11. **Lorie Lee Pike** on August 8, 1981 married **Robert William Sturgeon** (b. August 30, 1954 d.   ) son of William & Theresa Day Sturgeon of Cornish, ME. They had 2 children:

12. Michael David	b. April 3, 1984	d.
12. Andrea Lynn	b. December 30, 1985	d.

Lorie & Robert divorced in 1997.
Lorie on October 3, 1999 married **Rodney Lee Gilpatrick** (b. October 20, 1956 d. October 30, 2015) son of Erland LeRoy & Maude Sue Woodman Gilpatrick of Parsonsfield, ME. Lorie & Rodney had no children.

11. **David Wyer Pike** on June 21, 1986 married **Denise Livernois** (b. March 4, 1953 d.   ) daughter of Leon & Mary LeBoutillier Livernois of Southbridge, MA. They had 2 children:

12. Chad Robert	b. February 4, 1987	d.
12. Katherine Lee	b. February 13, 1988	d.

11. **Elizabeth Godfrey Tucker** on May 20, 1984 married **Dr Geoffrey David Gould** (b. October 11, 1939 d.   ) son of David Winfield & Grace (Hendrickson) Gould of Minneapolis, MN. They had 1 child:

12. Peter Coryell	b. April 25, 1985	d.

11. **Sarah Lowell Tucker** on August 28, 1989 married **David John Owens** (b. February 1, 1941 d.   ) son of David C & Iona (Pomeroy) Owens of Utica, NY. Sarah & David had no children & divorced in 2001.

11. **Margaret Sayre Tucker** on June 23, 1978 married **William Charles Mitchell Jr** (b. September 7, 1952 d.   ) son of William Charles & Helen (Yates) Mitchell of Louisville, KY. They had 3 children:

12. Andrew Russell	b. February 7, 1983	d.
12. Susan Anne	b. September 18, 1986	d.
12. Brian Thomas	b. September 11, 1989	d.

11. **Susan Seabury Hays** on May 31, 1980 married **Daniel James Whalen** (b. June 9, 1949 d.   ) son of David James & Virginia Frances (Evers) Whalen of Tomahawk, WI. They had 2 children:

12. James David	b. August 4, 1984	d.
12. Thomas Hopkins	b. December 12, 1987	d.

11. **David Libby Hays** on February 13, 2005 married **Anna Roth** (b. February 26, 1959 d.   ) daughter of Henry & Sylvia Ellen (Grossberg) Roth of S. Nyack, NY. They had 2 children:

    12. Benjamin Maxwell   b. August 2, 2006   d.

    12. Will McGowen   b. August 2, 2006   d.

11. **Daniel McGowan Hays** on February 19, 1984 married **Ludmila Borisovna** (b. June 7, 1956 d.   ) daughter of Boris Alexendrovich & Nina Nikolaevna (Ukhova) Borisovna of Leningrad, USSR. Daniel & Ludmila had no children & divorced in November 1991.

11. **Nancy Carol Lord**

11. **Susan Diane Lord** on August 30, 1969 married **David Alan Dixon** (b. August 18, 1940 d. September 2, 1982) son of Ralph Edwin & Ruth (Conley) Dixon of Battle Creek, MI. They had 3 children:

    12. Diane Lynne   b. December 19, 1971   d.

    12. Aimee Leigh   b. March 14, 1975   d.

    12. Audre Ruth   b. October 14, 1981   d.

11. **Donna Jeanne Lord** on July 4, 1993 married **Joseph Hussey Kendall** (b. June 11, 1949 d.   ) son of Leon Ellsworth & Barbara May (Hussey) Kendall of Cornish, ME. He had 2children in a previous union.

    12. Ryan Joseph   b. October 12, 1983   d.

    12. Angela Mae   b. October 6, 1986   d.

Donna Jeanne & Joseph had no children.

11. **Geoffrey Stacy Lord** on November 27, 1968 married **Janet Irene Jepson** (b. September 21, 1950 d.   ) daughter of Oscar Lester & Elaine (Parker) Jepson of Berwick, ME. Geoff & Janet had no children & divorced in June 1980.

    Geoff on August 23, 1980 married **Ellen Douglas McCausland** (b. September 4, 1959 d.   ) daughter of Thomas & Jean (Black) McCausland of Monkton, MD. Geoff & Ellen had no children.

11. **Joseph Merrill Lord** on October 4, 1975 married **Susan Holly Ripley** (b. December 23, 1952 d. daughter of Claire Edward & Beverly Madeline (Weeks) Ripley of Sheepscot, ME. They had 1 child:

    12. Josieda Marie "Sadie"   b. February 6, 1982   d.

J Merrill & Susan divorced in October 1991.

    J Merrill on August 1, 1992 married **Candace Rogers** (b. April 18, 1960 d.   ) daughter of Theodore Alan & Jane (Allen) Rogers of Port Townsend, WA. They had 1 child:

    12. Calvin Ambrose   b. December 9, 1993   d.

J Merrill & Candace divorced in 1997.

    J Merrill on March 28, 1998 married **Shelley Gravino** (b. September 27, 1959 d.   ) daughter of Guido Dominec & Evelyn Ruth (Giardina) Gravino of Niagara Falls, NY. J Merrill & Shelley had no children.

11. **Robyn Jeanne Lord** on September 30, 1989 married **Richard Allen Austin** (b. August 16, 1956 d.   ) son of Richard Henry & Carol Jane (White) Austin of Nashua, NH. They had 2 children:

    12. Molly Lord   b. December 18, 1991   d.

    12. Max Philip   b. January 19, 1994   d.

Robyn & Richard divorced in 2001.

Robyn on February 25, 2007 married **Paul Allen Nichols** (b. July 27, 1966 d.   ) son of George Allen & Martha Ann (Martin) Nichols of Rome, GA. Robyn & Paul had no children.

11. **Dana Wadleigh Lord** on December 11, 1993 married **Shirley Dagmar Zeisberg** (b. January 19, 1950 d.   ) from Germany. Dana & Shirley had no children.

11. **Alan David Lord** on December 29, 1990 married **Anne Clemens Hendershott** (b. July 8, 1959 d.   ) daughter of Charles & Jacquelynn (Vizzini) Hendershott of New Orleans, LA. Alan & Anne had no children & divorced on February 3, 1994.

Alan on December 17, 1994 married **Margaret Knott** "Margi" (b. October 6, 1959 d.   ) daughter of Sydney Tucker Jr & Ruth Ellen (Senate) Knott of Barnstable, MA. Alan & Margaret had no children.

11. **Leigh Ann Bonney** on September 9, 2000 married **Larry Ritzhaupt** (b. March 10, 1949 d.   ) son of Delbert Samuel & Iva Louise (Britton) Ritzhaupt of Galion, OH. Leigh & Larry had no children.

11. **Jonathan Daniel Lord** on August 6, 1988 married **Jill Marie Christofferson** (b. April 1, 1955 d.   ) daughter of Robert Stanley & Grace Irene (Smith) Christofferson of Hibbing, MN. They had 1 child:

    12. Jonathan Daniel Jr. "Daniel"   b. March 6, 1989   d.

11. **Jay Merrill Lord II** on October 27, 1990 married **Priscilla Ann Sawyer** (b. March 14, 1962 d.   ) daughter of Jeremy Jason & Barbara (Harmon)Sawyer of Hampton, NH. They had 1 child:

    12. Calvin Merrill   b. December 22, 1992   d.

11. **David Kimball Lord**

11. **Nathan Andrew Fates** on June 10, 2000 married **Corey Patricia Pike** (b. January 19, 1973 d.   ) daughter of Kenneth Thorton & Paula Marie (Powers) Pike of South Portland, ME. They had 1 child:

    12. Sophia Sage   b. December 21, 2005   d.

Nathan & Corey divorced on December 8, 2017.

11. **Justin Joshua Faatz** on August 27, 2005 married **Sarah Rosalind Rogers** (b. May 31, 1975 d.   ) daughter of Scott Guy & Vicki Ray (Porter) Rogers of Unity, ME. They had 2 children:

    12. Joshua Nicholas   b. April 22, 2007   d.

    12. Anna Elizabeth   b. May 25, 2010   d.

11. **Robyn Dayle Pettengill** on September 25, 2004 married **Dana Violette** (b. November 6, 1965 d.   ) son of Marcel Sr. & Roberta Jean (Paulsen) Violette, of Cumberland, ME Robyn & Dana had no children & divorced on August 16, 2017.

11. **Jennifer Lord Pettengill** on October 5, 1996 married **Jay Kenneth Banks** (b. August 5, 1964 d.   )
     son of Harland William & Betty Lou (Dodge) Banks of Gorham, ME They had 4 children:

    12. Jackson Audway   b. June 1, 1999   d.

    12. Georgia Elizabeth   b. January 12, 2001   d.

    12. Griffin William   b. November 27, 2002   d.

    12. Jay Hudson   b. April 24, 2008   d.

Jennifer & Jay divorced January 2, 2012.

11. **Sarah Churchill Treworgy** on June 29, 2002 married **John de LaChapelle** (b. October 15, 1961
     d.   ) son of Richard Passerat & Patricia Ruth (Fisher) de LaChapelle of Oak Harbor, WA. They
     had 2 children:

    12. Finn Stuart   b September 9, 2005   d.

    12. Jack Edward   b. July 31, 2008   d.

11. **Hannah Bigelow Treworgy** on February 28, 2005 married **George Ekwere** (b. May 25, 1976 d.   )
     son of Joseph Ekwere & Magrete Luma of Limbe, South West Province, Cameroon. They had 1 child:

    12. Jasper Bigelow   b. June 24, 2009   d.

Hannah & George divorced November 4, 2016.

11. **Samantha Lenard Aigner-Treworgy**

11. **Adam Scott Aigner-Treworgy** on September 5, 2015 married **Susan Joyce Davis** (b. November 10,
     1979 d.   ) daughter of Gerald Vincent & Anne Veronica (Torpey) Davis of Philadelphia, PA.

12. **Spencer Charles Churchill**

12. **Jason Steven Coates**

12. **Eric Joseph Seamans**

12. **Jeffrey Allen Stocks** on July 7, 2001 married **Rebecca Joy McNeil** (b. August 21, 1978 d.   )
     daughter of Gary Wayne & Brenda Louise (Howe) McNeil of Baldwin, ME. They had 2 children:

    13. Isaac Timothy   b. June 4, 2002   d.

    13. Caleb Andrew   b. February 21, 2005   d.

Jeff & Rebecca divorced in 2007.

12. **Christopher Stocks** had 2 children with **Michelle Perkins** (b. August 21, 1978 d.   ) daughter of
     Westley Thomas & Cynthia Rosa (Shaw) Perkins of Portland, ME.

    13. Olivia Rosana   b. April 16, 1997   d.

    13. Dylan Christopher   b. September 6, 2004   d.

12. **Cass Randolph Churchill** had 1 child with **Elizabeth Pierie** (b. November 7, 1986 d.   ) daughter
     of Lawrence & Jodie (Thiriault) Pierie of Portland, ME.

    13. Emma Jean   b. September 14, 2012

12. **Alexis Catherine Jade Ives**

12. **Stuart Nicholas Henry Ives**

12. **Eric Samuel David Ives**

12. **Alexandra Leigh Black**

12. **Carson James Black**

12. **Michael David Sturgeon** on September 1, 2012 married **Heidi Sinclair Morrill** (b. June 27, 1985 d.   ) daughter of Dan Andrew & Laurie Ann (Crommet) Morrill of Cornish, ME. They had 1 child:
    13. Reese Caroline   b. September 23. 2014   d.
    13 Maci Jane   b. January 19, 2018   d.

12. **Andrea Lynn Sturgeon** on September 20, 2014 married **Joshua Brian Emmons** (b. February 22, 1985 d.   ) son of Terry G & Celeste Ann (Beleckis) Emmons of Denmark, ME. They had 1 child:
    13. Daniel Robert   b. October 29. 2015   d.

12. **Chad Robert Pike** on August 20, 2016 married **Renee Sarah Daigle** (b. January 29, 1986 d.   ) daughter of Richard Aurel & Joan (Cumberland) Daigle of Madawaska, ME.

12. **Katherine Lee Pike**

12. **Peter Coryell Gould** on July 20, 2018 married **Elizabeth Anne Francis** (b. December 29, 1991 d.   ) daughter of John Leroy & Kelley (Sax) Francis of Johnson City, NH.

12. **Andrew Russell Mitchell** on April 17, 2013 married **Rebecca Catherine Riggs** (b. February 16, 1990 d.   ) daughter of Christopher Thomas & Glenda Rachel Hill (Evers) Riggs of Westcliffe, CO. They had 2 children:
    13. Jack William   b. September 1, 2013   d.
    13. Grace Tucker   b. June 28, 2016   d.

12. **Susan Anne Mitchell** on July 14, 2009 married **Matthew Joseph Miller** (b. January 4, 1987 d.   ) son of Mark Miller & Molly (Tate) Matheny of Nashville, TN. They had 1 child:
    13. Lilly Anne   b. December 17, 2009   d.

12. **Brian Thomas Mitchell** on May 28, 2016 married **Lindsey Tenneson** (b. August 21, 1990 d.   ) daughter of

12. **James David Whalen**

12. **Thomas Hopkins Whalen** on August 8, 2014 married **Abby Louise Blinkhorn** (b. August 28, 1983 d.   ) daughter of William & Marilyn (Helena) Blinkhorn of Portland, ME

12. **Benjamin Maxwell Hays**

12. **Will McGowan Hays**

12. **Diane Lynne Dixon** on July 10, 1999 married **Donald Wesley Underwood** (b. November 10, 1971 d.   ) son of Donald Lloyd & Carolyn (Caldwell) Underwood of Gobles, MI. They had 2 children:

13. Gibson David	b. May 14, 2001	d.
13. Baxter Donald	b. July 22, 2006	d. July 22, 2006

12. **Aimee Leigh Dixon** had 1 child by **Ronald Dean Burgess** son of Ronald Elbert & Pauline Elizabeth (Lynch) Burgess of Nederland, CO

13. Sadira Nadine Burgess	b. August 7, 2000	d.

Aimee on September 18, 2010 married **Randall Mark Staples** (b. July 2, 1959 d.   ) son of Mark Paul & Jeaneen Atlantis (Senjem) Staples of Star Prairie, WI. Aimee & Randall had no children.

12. **Audre Ruth Dixon** on August 8, 2017 married **Ronald Raymond Rabb Jr** (b. May 4, 1981 d.   ) son of Ronald Raymond Sr & Suzanne Pearl (Moser) Rabb of Kalamazoo, MI They had 2 children:

13. Lucius Raymond	b. December 4, 2011	d.
13. Wyleigh Jay	b. September 20, 2013	d.

12. **Josieda Marie Lord** on July 7, 2018 married **Kyle Robert Pettit** (b. October 7, 1984 d.   ) son of Donald Richard & Jo Ann (Parker) Pettit of Santa Rosa, CA

12. **Calvin Ambrose Lord**

12. **Molly Lord Austin**

12. **Max Phillip Austin**

12. **Jonathan Daniel Lord, Jr**

12. **Calvin Merrill Lord**

12. **Sophia Sage Fates**

12. **Joshua Nicholas Faatz**

12. **Anna Elizabeth Faatz**

12. **Jackson Audway Banks**

12. **Georgia Elizabeth Banks**

12. **Griffin William Banks**

12. **Jay Hudson Banks**

12. **Finn Stuart de LaChapelle**

12. **Jack Edward de LaChapelle**

12. **Jasper Bigelow Ekwere**

13. **Makaila Rayne Curtis**

13. **Isaac Timothy Stocks**

13. **Caleb Andrew Stocks**

13. **Olivia Rosana Stocks**

13. **Dylan Christopher Stocks**

13. **Emma Jean Churchill**

13. **Reese Caroline Sturgeon**

13. **Daniel Robert Emmons**

13. **Jack William Mitchell**

13. **Grace Tucker Mitchell**

13. **Lilly Anne Miller**

13. **Gibson David Underwood**

13. **Baxter Donald Underwood** never married or had children

13. **Sadira Nadine Burgess**

13. **Lucius Raymond Rabb**

13. **Wyleigh Jay Rabb**

DESCENDANTS OF JOHN C CHURCHILL & ANNIE BURK

7. **John C Churchill** on October 18, 1869 married **Annie Burk** (b. September 5, 1846 d. February 22, 1917) daughter of William H & Ann Eulalie (Calbeck) Burk of E Boston, MA. They had 4 children:

8. Frank Percy	b. November 24, 1872	d. July 24, 1954
8. Preston Banks	b. April 21, 1876	d. September 22, 1956
8. Lindsey Walter	b. December 18, 1881	d. August 20, 1955
8. Eulalie	b. April 5, 1883	d. January 6, 1935

8. **Frank Percy Churchill** on July 16, 1899 married **Florence K Daniels** (b. 1870 d. 1950) daughter of Charles & Isabelle Daniels of Providence, RI. Frank & Florence had no children.

8. **Preston Banks Churchill** on October 3, 1900 married **Edythe Blaisdell** (b. November 22, 1876 d. February 26, 1964) daughter of Andrew M & Ella (Crawford) Blaisdell of Brunswick, ME. They had 1 child:

9. Lindsey Crawford	b. January 4, 1903	d. July 3, 1961

8. **Lindsey Walter Churchill** never married or had children.

8. **Eulalie Churchill** never married or had children.

9. **Lindsey Crawford Churchill** on January 29, 1929 married **Vieno Mary Kajander** (b. December 21, 1903 d. June 4, 1964) daughter of Jack & Mary Laurila Kajander of Fitchburg, MA. They had 2 children:

10. Lindsey Crawford Jr	b. August 10, 1935	d.
10. John Preston	b. October 30, 1939	d.

10. **Lindsey Crawford Churchill, Jr** on July 7, 1957 married **Roberta Gail Lester** (b. September 29, 1933 d.   ) daughter of Leonard & Shirley (Siegel) Lester of Roslyn, NY. They had 2 children:

11. Dana Lester	b. January 5, 1961	d.
11. Lauren Sarah "Laurie"	b. September 18, 1964	d.

10. **John Preston Churchill** on August 19, 1967 married **Faith Anne Scalise** (b. April 13, 1941 d.   ) daughter of James Joseph & Adeline Lillian (Marinelli) Scalise of New Britain, CT. They had 2 children:

11. Anne Elizabeth	b. February 25, 1969	d.
11. Alison Jane	b. April 7, 1972	d.

11. **Dana Lester Churchill** on July 6, 2003 married **Wei Wang** (b. July 23, 1962 d.   ) daughter of Yongfu & Yunzhi (Zhou) Wang of Dandong, Liaoning, China. Wei had a child in a previous union.

      12. Wayne Zhang   b. March 16, 1986   d.

    Dana & Wei had no children.

11. **Lauren Sarah Churchill**

11. **Anne Elizabeth Churchill**

11. **Alison Jane Churchill** on July 14, 2007 married **Michael Klezos** (b. March 1, 1971 d. July 7, 2010) son of Stanley & Linda Grace (Wood) Klezos of W. Hartford, CT. Alison & Michael had no children.

DESCENDANTS OF MARY RELIANCE CHURCHILL & NEHEMIAH TOWLE LIBBY

7. **Mary Reliance Churchill** on February 21, 1860 married **Nehemiah Towle Libby** (b. September 20, 1837 d. May 23, 1887) son of Isaac & Roxanna (Towle) Libby of Porter, ME. They had 2 children:

8. Emma A	b. November 2, 1862	d. 1892
8. Walter Day	b. November 8, 1864	d. August 6, 1941

8. **Emma A Libby** on January 30, 1887 married **Oscar F Wiggin** (b. 1857 d. July 4, 1887) son of Jacob & Rose A (Mason) Wiggin. Emma & Oscar had no children.
   Emma in 1890 married **Edgar Francis Gentleman** (b. April 29, 1860 d. September 18, 1943) son of William Francis & Diana A (Wilkerson) Gentleman of Porter ME. They had 1 child:

9. Merton Eugene	b. August 16, 1891	d. August 11, 1979

8. **Walter Day Libby** on June 16, 1889 married **Flora Lillian Hubbard** (b. October 22, 1871 d. March 19, 1937) daughter of Charles & Flora (Wadsworth) Hubbard of Hiram, ME. They had 2 children:

9. Harold Weston	b. August 17, 1892	d. April 9, 1972
9. Carleton Glen	b. February 6, 1894	d. November 26, 1956

9. **Merton Eugene Gentleman** on July 13, 1924 married **Ava Magdalene Barnett** (b. March 5, 1898 d. July 6, 1991) daughter of William Skyler & Sarah (Fields) Barnett of Glen Elder, KS. They had 2 children:

10. Merton Eugene Jr	b. November 9, 1925	d.
10. Lawrence B	b. June 15, 1931	d. July 2, 2015

9. **Harold Weston Libby** on October 25, 1916 married **Marie Ona McClun** (b. April 11, 1893 d. September 23, 1925) daughter on John C & Elizabeth (Cribbs) McClun of Cawker City, KS. Harold & Marie had no children.

9. **Carleton Glen Libby** on September 4, 1920 married **Dorothy Elizabeth Norris** (b. February 5, 1896 d. November 25, 1991) daughter of Sidney Rendall & Maude (Whittelsey) Norris of Topeka, KS. They had 2 children:

10. Shirley Jeanne	b. October 7, 1922	d. March 5, 2002
10. Carolyn Lou	b. July 4, 1932	d.

10. **Merton Eugene Gentleman Jr** on May 2, 1954 married **Charlotte Louise Maynard** (b. March 26, 1926 d. November 12, 2009) daughter of Reed Lewis & Anna (Cubbinson) Maynard of Beloit, KS. They had 2 children:

11. Duane Eugene	b. February 2, 1956	d.
11. Lynn Olin	b. October 11, 1958	d.

10. **Lawrence B Gentleman** on March 21, 1954 married **Betty Lou Thiessen** (b. December 2, 1934 d.   ) daughter of Ernest C & Anna (Schmeil) Thiessen of Beloit, KS. They had 2 children:

11. Sharon Kay	b. October 5, 1956	d.
11. Kathryn Jo	b. June 11, 1960	d.

10. **Shirley Jeanne Libby** on June 11, 1946 married **John Bunyan Smith, Jr** (b. January 9, 1916 d. April 2, 1981) son of John Bunyan Sr & Mary (Lilly) Smith of Jacksonville, FL. They had 2 children:

11. Carolyn Sue	b. September 21, 1948	d.
11. Sharon Ann	b. September 18, 1951	d.

Shirley on July 26, 1984 married **Frank G Love** (b. October 7, 1922 d.   ) son of John & Eola Love of Lafayette, LA. Shirley & Frank had no children.

10. **Carolyn Lou Libby** on October 18, 1949 married **Edwin Lamar Dennis Jr** (b. June 29, 1926 d. August 27, 2012) son of Edwin Lamar Sr & Maurice (Gormandy) Dennis of Baton Rouge, LA. They had 2 children:

11. Adele Lynn	b. January 11, 1954	d.
11. Laura Leigh	b. February 1, 1955	d.

11. **Duane Eugene Gentleman** on June 16, 1978 married **Cheryl Diane Powell** (b. June 12, 1956 d.   ) daughter of Donald & Bonnie Powell of Ottawa, KS. They had 2 childrern:

12. Sarah Diane	b. March 8, 1985	d.
12. Nathan Eugene	b. March 22, 1992	d.

11. **Lynn Olin Gentleman**

11. **Sharon Kay Gentleman** on July 19, 1975 married **James David Kindscher** (b. November 7, 1955 d.   ) son of John Jacob & Doris (James) Kindscher of Beloit, KS. They had 2 children:

12. Lauren Raissa	b. April 16, 1981	d.
12. Allison Kay	b. February 11, 1984	d.

Sharon & James divorced in 1984.

Sharon on September 13, 1993 married **John C Fuller** (b. September 10, 1945 d.   ) son of Ansell C & Polly (Spain) Fuller of Beloit, KS.

11. **Kathryn Jo Gentleman** on July 18, 1981 married **David Bruce Grabbe** (b. March 3, 1956 d.   ) son of Clarence & Lillian Grabbe of Hays, KS. They had 2 children:

12. Cody Taylor	b. November 17, 1985	d.
12. Kaylee Brynn	b. May 24, 1988	d.

11. **Carolyn Sue Smith** on April 20, 1974 married **Martin Anthony Petrich III** (b. December 21, 1942 d.   ) son of Martin Anthony Jr & Jean (Clark) Petrich of Lafayette, LA. They had 2 children:

    12. Benjamin Clark   b. April 6, 1977   d.

    12. Ian Norris   b. October 29, 1980   d.

11. **Sharon Ann Smith** on November 22, 1979 married **Curley James Darby** (b. December 9, 1948 d.   ) son of Leroy Joseph & Emily (Smith) Darby of Lafayette, LA. They had 2 children:

    12. Luke William   b. December 1, 1986   d.

    12. Kelly Carolyn   b. February 6, 1990   d.

11. **Adele Lynne Dennis** on August 7, 1976 married **David Patrick White** (b. December 13, 1952 d.   ) son of Patrick William & Mary (Jones) White of Virginia Beach, VA. They had 2 children:

    12. Christopher David   b. September 2, 1984   d.

    12. Courtney Lynn Adele   b. December 9, 1986   d.

11. **Laura Leigh Dennis** on December 29, 1982 married **Jack Moulton Schmidt** (b. February 1, 1955 d.   ) son of Jack & Gladys Schmidt of Virginia Beach, VA. They had 2 children:

    12. Jennifer Libby   b. August 25, 1985   d.

    12. Jessica Ingrid   b. July 25, 1989   d.

12. **Sarah Diane Gentleman**

12. **Nathan Eugene Gentleman**

12. **Lauren Raissa Kindscher**

12. **Allison Kay Kindscher**

12. **Cody Taylor Grabbe**

12. **Kaylee Brynn Grabbe**

12. **Benjamin Clark Petrich**

12. **Ian Norris Petrich**

12. **Luke William Darby**

12. **Kelly Carolyn Darby**

12. **Christopher David White**

12. **Courtney Lynn Adele White**

12. **Jennifer Libby Schmidt**

12. **Jessica Ingrid Schmidt**

Part Two:
Biographies, stories, and reminiscences

Phyllis Evelyn Lord and dog Mack Sennet

NATHAN LORD

Adapted from *A History of the Descendants of Nathan Lord of Ancient Kittery, Me.,* compiled by C.C Lord, arranged for publication by George E. Lord. Concord, N.H.: The Rumford Press, 1912.

Nathan came to New England in 1636 with Abraham Conley on the *Elizabeth and Ann*. Nathan is first found in Kittery, Maine, in 1652, when he signed an agreement acknowledging Massachusetts as having judicial authority in Maine. The first permanent English settlement in Maine had begun in the 1620s, when Fernando Gorges and John Mason received joint title to the land and began settlements. In 1677, Massachusetts purchased the Gorges' lands from Fernando's heirs, and in 1691, Maine was incorporated as part of Massachusetts.

The land system in early New England was an important factor in holding a community together. Under this system a company of applicants to the legislature, perhaps a fragment of a church congregation, was granted a "plantation right," which authorized a settlement in a designated region just beyond the existing frontier line. If, in the passing of a year or two the experiment proved successful, they were given a "town right." This allowed them not only full representation in the general court but the common proprietorship of the land, which was at this time precisely bounded. Much of the land was held in common and regulated by town ordinances. Individual holdings were assigned by selected representatives. Since magistrates and ministers were given larger plots, it was an advantage to be elected magistrate. Judging by the number of early settlers who became elected magistrates, many families earned extra land in this manner.

Nathan, a planter, received his first land grant in Kittery on December 16, 1652. The grant comprised 60 acres. Nathan was involved in land transactions in ancient Kittery a number of times. One interesting exchange in 1676 involved Richard Nason, who sold Nathan nine acres of land in Berwick in return for a horse of the "culler Sorrell" with a white star on its forehead. Court records list Nathan as being involved in land transfers that also affected Abraham Conley, Miles Thompson, and Thomas Abbot, all members of families that intermarried with the Lords. In June 1678, Nathan and his second wife Martha sold land on Sturgeon Creek formerly belonging to Abraham Conley. In September 1679, the court had to settle a dispute between Nathan and Nicholas Frost over a piece of land that had formerly been the Conley's.

In March 1690/91, Abraham Conley's will of March 1, 1674 was presented in court. It named his son-in-law Nathan Lord as executor and left bequests to Nathan and two of his sons Nathan and Abraham, who were to receive their bequests when they turned 21.

The Lord Garrison was located in the district known as Oldfields in South Berwick. It was maintained during the Indian troubles and used as a residence into the early 1800's. The garrison was a unique and extensive edifice and had a door through which could be driven a yoke of oxen and cart. The door was surmounted by a carved figurehead which represented the prow of a ship. Many carvings on its interior added to its adornment.

Administration of Nathan's estate was granted to his widow Martha in 1690/91. Martha, as administrator of Nathan's Estate, sued Nicholas Morrill for trespassing and for holding land belonging to the estate. The case involved 14 acres of land, originally granted to Abraham Conley that had been bequeathed to Nathan and Martha's sons, Abraham and Samuel. The court records show that Martha and her grandson, William (Abraham's son), had agreed to a division.

JOSEPH MERRILL LORD

by Joanne Libby, 1944

In a little, old New England farmhouse about 40 miles from Portland in the small country town of Parsonsfield, Maine, lived Josephine Merrill Lord and Daniel Lord, my grandparents. They had been married for several years and had always wanted a child. Finally, on October 29, 1865, a healthy, bouncing boy was born and named after careful deliberation, Joseph Merrill Lord I. Young Merrill was a chubby, towheaded, good-natured baby, whom his mother adored; he might have been spoiled if it hadn't been for the birth of his sister, Hattie, when he was almost 2 years old. As she grew older, she became his constant companion and playmate. One of their favorite playgrounds in the summer was in the pasture across the road from the house where there were various small brooks in which boats could be sailed and where they could wade to their hearts content. In the winter during the days when they weren't in school, they would slide on the crisp snow with their homemade sleds in the fields in back of the house.

His early education was acquired in a little red schoolhouse about a mile from his home. In the middle of the winter, it was very difficult to get to school, but he missed very few days. There was a time in March and April called MUD TIME, when traveling of any kind was very difficult until the frost came out of the ground and the mud began to dry up. Young Merrill showed an aptitude for using tools and during his spare time amused himself making various gadgets such as water wheels for the brook and toys for his little sister who idolized him.

His mother was very proud of him and early on made up her mind that her son was of higher intelligence than other boys around and that he was to be a professional man. When he was older, he was to be given the choice of studying to be a doctor or a lawyer. In those days, a professional man was held in higher esteem than a man who did a trade or farming.

As time went on, he and Hattie completed their educations in the "town school" as the grade schools were called in those days. Because Merrill was a fine student and a book lover, Hattie was inspired to work harder; therefore she finally caught up to him and entered high school in the same class.

In the meantime, when Merrill was 12 years old, his father died and for a time he was the man of the house. A few months afterwards, Elisha Wadleigh, who lived on a neighboring farm, began to court Josephine and the courtship ended in marriage. Merrill and Hattie found themselves leaving their childhood home and moving into Elisha Wadleigh's lovely big farmhouse. It became Merrill's home for the rest of his life.

The high school that they attended is now known as Parsonsfield Seminary. At that time, it was called Parsonsfield Academy and Piper Free High School. During that time the school was held with one term at North Parsonsfield, one term at East Parsonsfield, and one term in Kezar Falls. There were no special courses then like we have now: they just took up the general subjects. These included Reading, Writing, History, Math, Latin, Greek, and Science. There were different towns located four miles in different directions from Merrill's house and he and Hattie had to walk this distance every day except the worst days in winter. Then Elisha would hitch up his horse and sleigh and take them to school. In this way, they completed their courses and graduated together in the Class of 1887.

Joseph was a very brilliant student with a deep analytical mind and was always near the head of the class. If there were any pranks being played, he was seldom among the active participants, but if you checked back, you would probably find that he had a big share in the planning. He was not so much interested in girls as most boys of that age but apparently preferred books and studying. This might possibly be due to the fact that he was reserved and naturally shy. However, before he graduated from "Par-Seminary," he met a very attractive, vivacious young lady by the name of Sarah Churchill, who seemed to have all the qualities that he lacked and he became intensely attracted to her. Merrill's mother definitely approved of this match because Sarah evidently had the social qualities that a lawyer's wife would need. At this time, he had decided to become a lawyer to please his mother whom he adored. Sarah had plenty of beaus and although Merrill attracted her somewhat, she wasn't ready to settle down yet. She loved to dance, sing, and be gay. Merrill couldn't dance a step or sing a note and didn't know how to be gay. Thus, it seemed that in spite of his mother's wishes for a mutual attraction, the vivacious Sarah could never tie herself down to anyone as quiet and steady as Merrill. Thus, the romance stood when he entered Boston University to take up the study of law. By working very hard, he finished his law course in three years and graduated in the Class of 1890 with the degree of Bachelor of Laws. Upon the completion of his course at the university he became a member of the faculty of that institution, teaching the subjects of real property and contracts. Also in 1890, he was admitted to the Suffolk County Bar. That same year his life was saddened by the death of his beloved sister. It was thought that her life had been shortened by overtaxing her strength in trying to keep up with her older brother in school.

Being a native of Maine and realizing he would be going back there he eventually applied for admission to the York County Bar and was accepted as a member.

Doubtless, due to the fact that "absence makes the heart grow fonder," the attraction between Sarah and Merrill which had started in high school developed into a real romance. On a lovely day in August 1893, their very attractive wedding took place on the piazza of the home of his stepfather, Elisha Wadleigh. Escorted by their friends and relatives, who were well equipped with rice and old shoes, the young couple went to Cornish, Maine and took a train to Massachusetts where Merrill had an apartment ready for his bride.

J. Merrill and Sarah Lord

During the school year 1893-1894 the young couple led a most interesting and colorful life. Josephine was right when she thought that Sarah would be a social asset to Merrill's career. She loved people and they loved her. Their home became a center of gaiety and laughter. They made many delightful friends during their short stay in Massachusetts and most of the friendships lasted throughout their lives.

In 1894, Merrill was called home by the death of his mother. Elisha's big house being without a mistress, Merrill thought it was his duty to move back there for good. His sister Hattie had been married right out of high school and upon her death left a daughter Hattie, whom Elisha and Josephine had been taking care of. It now became Sarah's duty to mother the young six-year-old Hattie whose father had died two years before.

Merrill looked around for a good place for his law office and finally decided on Limerick, Maine which was nine miles away. In those days the only means of transportation was the horse and buggy, and certain days of the week he went this distance to take care of his law clients. He never cared much for driving horses as his mind was always occupied with deeper things, but it was something he had to do so he did it.

In November 1894, a daughter was born to Sarah and Merrill and she was christened Theresa Churchill. In spite of the fact that Merrill had studied law and was developing into a successful lawyer, it would not have been his choice if his mother hadn't desired it so strongly. He would have chosen the field of electrical engineering. Because he was trained in the profession of law he earned his living for himself and his family from his legal practice. Nevertheless, that didn't prevent him from studying or practicing his hobby of electrical engineering on the side. He was especially interested in the telephone which was just being developed. He was the founder of the Ossipee Valley Telegraph and Telephone Company, which was the first telephone company in that section and later became a branch of New England Telephone and Telegraph Company. He made his own first telephone with cigar boxes, and the line went from the living room to the shop upstairs. Later, the switchboard was in the living room, and at one time he had a full time operator to take care of the calls.

In 1897, his first son was born and was Frank Wadleigh.

In 1899, he was the superintendent of the schools, a task that he enjoyed very much, for he was very interested in developing the minds of young people. That same year another son arrived. He was Myron Otis.

In Limerick, about this time, there was a man, Frank Fenderson, about 10 years younger than Merrill who had completed the study of law and was looking for an office in which to practice. Merrill was very much interested in giving a lift to this worthy, young man. Believing this particular young man was capable, he took him into his office to read law. His judgment was correct, for eventually the law firm became Lord and Fenderson and the two became close friends and had sincere respects for each other's abilities. Although J Merrill Lord I, as he was now known, was a lawyer of unusual ability, he cared little for the work of the trial court and gradually withdrew from this branch of practice and gave his entire time to the settlement of estates and corporation law.

He was also interested in a local lumber company and became one of the large stock holders and directors.

In 1901, his third son, Daniel Bertram was born and in 1909, a daughter, Phyllis Evelyn was born. This completed his family of five children.

J Merrill's and Sarah's lives were as near a perfect championship as possible in this life. The fun-loving Sarah was always attracting crowds. During the summer vacations the friends and relatives were delighted to come to the Lord Farm and received a cordial welcome. It was not unusual during these periods to feed 25 people at a meal. The atmosphere was relaxed, comfortable and happy at all times. The people who came once almost invariably wished to come back again and again. Sarah was a born hostess and delighted to be surrounded with her friends for indefinite periods. J Merrill enjoyed the crowds too, in spite of the fact that he was more quiet and reserved.

In between whiles, he had built up the farm and fully equipped it with pigs, cows, horses, sheep, and once he experimented with squabs for the market. He was always interested in the new scientific developments and his farm was the first one in the area to have acetylene lights and a bathroom. Also, he was the first in town to have a car. It was one of the first Stanley Steamers and the family felt very proud to go riding in it. He always could drive his own cars but didn't care much about it as his mind was too occupied with deeper things. He and Sarah instilled in their children a liking for the simple things of life and taught them how to live successfully. A richer heritage could not be given to anyone.

Because of his liking for young people, he started many local boys on the road to success in the scientific world. A young cousin of his, Wilbur Merrill, who became the head of the Works Laboratory of General Electric Company in Schenectady, New York, owes his successful career to the encouragement and assistance given to him by J. Merrill Lord I.

J. Merrill was a man of vision, and because of that he set out apple orchards in every available spot on the farm while the boys were small and taught them the value of such a project. As a result, the boys reaped the benefits of his foresight.

Because he was a great reader and great student, he was interested in schools and wanted the best education attainable for his children and other people's children. He was particularly interested in "Par-Seminary." He was on the Board of Trustees and the Board of Education and worked very hard to make the school flourish and prosperous. He always kept in close touch with the teachers and became a real friend with nearly all the principals during his life. They respected his opinions and judgments, and he was always willing to help out wherever he could with advice, suggestions, and actual work.

He never did much physical work himself, but he had a way of getting other people to do it for him and making them like it. There were always hired men around the place, some of them living there, and for years he would give a high school student a chance to work for his room and board when the boy felt he couldn't afford to live in the dormitory. The students were all expected to be decent and honorable and do what was expected of them. They all lived up to it and many of them made the farm their home until they married or went into business for themselves.

As he grew older, he took an increasing interest in politics. In 1907, some of his friends thought he would be a good candidate for the State Legislature. At first, because of his shy and retiring nature he refused to run but finally he thought better of it and was elected. He found the weekly trips to Augusta so stimulating and the contacts he made so worthwhile, that in 1917 he ran for the office of State Senator from York County and was elected. He held this office at the time of his death. He was greatly esteemed by his fellow senators. A close friend, who knew him well, said that at least two governors of Maine had relied implicitly on the sound advice he had given them on many matters of state policy.

His manner was always quiet and reserved so that some people were a little afraid of him even though they had great respect for his ability. His children stood in awe of him and never tried the same tactics with him that had they tried with Sarah. In order to discipline them, all he had to do was look at them sternly and tell them what to do or what not to do, and his wishes were speedily carried out. His method of discipline was more effective than Sarah's spankings and scoldings. He was very generous with his family and gave them everything he could afford and some things he could not. The gifts were never foolish but were something either useful or educational.

Because of Sarah's gaiety and J Merrill's steadfastness and integrity, the home life they managed to give their children was one of the happiest of kin. It was a great factor in holding the family together. There were always fun, picnics, music, rides, and plenty of friends to fill in the spare time. There was plenty of work too, and each member of the family was expected to do his or her share, whatever it was, and to do it without grumbling. In this way, the family was taught not only to enjoy living but to earn the right to this enjoyment.

He was deeply religious and attended church regularly, insisting on the whole family going with him and staying for Sunday School. He had a deep philosophy of life that carried him over the hard places, leaving him stronger for the experience. He never smoked or drank any kind of liquor, but he liked good food. He often told his children never to be afraid to try a new dish because they might miss something good.

In addition to his many activities he had an insurance business at his home, which brought him in contact with people in the surrounding towns.

As he grew older, some of his investments became deeply involved, and the worry and the overwork necessary to control them caused him to develop a bad heart condition. For two years before his death, he was under a doctor's care, but being a very hard-working man, it was difficult to make him follow the doctor's orders, about rest and diet. One of his favorite foods was beefsteak, and the doctor prohibited all red meats. Once in a while, however, this craving would get the better of him, and he would indulge in a meal of steak. It was during such a dinner, on February 27, 1920, that his heart refused to carry the burden any longer, and while cutting the meat at the dinner table, he gave a gasp and lapsed into a coma and never regained consciousness. The whole county and part of the State were saddened by his death. It was a terrific blow to his family. They had not realized how much they leaned on him.

His sudden death left the family without its mainstay, and for a short time the situation seemed unbearable. Then gradually his boys began to show the qualities he instilled in them, and little by little they picked up the loose ends of his business interests and straightened out the entanglements.

I am proud to be the granddaughter of J. Merrill Lord I and am sorry I did not have the pleasure of knowing him personally.

Retyped by D. Kimball Lord, August 18, 1990
Edited by Donna Lord Kendall, May 6, 2018

Sarah and J. Merrill Lord

J. Merrill Lord

Sarah Churchill Lord

WILBUR LORIN MERRILL

by David Merrill Lord, April 4, 1955 for an English class at Gould Academy.

Brothers John and Nathaniel Merrill came from Salisbury, County Wilts, England to Ipswich, Massachusetts in 1633 and settled at Newbury in the same colony. They were among the first settlers of that town. They are descended from the Huguenot Family of DeMerle who escaped to England after the St Bartholomew Day (August 1572). This family of DeMerle belonged to the Auvergne nobility having had its ancestral estate near Place-de-Dombes in that province.

The emigrant Nathaniel made use of the arms we give which are different (although the crest is the same) from the Merrill arms as given by the English works of heraldry. We have seen imprints of the seal of one of the emigrants grandsons (Thomas Merrill 3, Abel 2, Nathaniel 1) affixed to a deed dated 1726. The devices were exactly those we give.

"ARMS - Argent, a bar azure between 3 peacocks' heads proper."

"CREST - A peacocks head erased, proper."

The above is quoted from America Heraldica.

(Ancestors of George W Merrill of Saginaw, MI by William Merrill, p. 1)

Joseph	1795 - 1889	age 90
Hardy	1818 - 1901	age 83
Abigil	1823 - 1905	age 82
Lorin	1854 - 1912	age 58
Wilbur	1879 - 1956	age 76

In a little old New England farmhouse, about forty-five miles west of Portland, in the small township of Parsonsfield, Maine, lived Lorin Hardy and Ida Jane Merrill with Lorin's father, Hardy Merrill. Their farm consisted of some 600 acres of land and housed 100 head of cattle. The Merrills were descendants of French Huguenots who called themselves Merle-French for blackbird.

On November 14, 1879, their first and only child was born to Lorin and Ida, and this son was named Wilbur Lorin Merrill.

Although Maine's "Bill Merrill Mountain," according to the best accounts, was named some years before the birth of Wilbur "Bill" Merrill, violent friends insist that the mountain was named in anticipation of this man.

From an early age, Wilbur showed extreme mechanical ability. This doubtlessly stemmed from the fact that his grandfather, Hardy Merrill, was a shipbuilder in Wiscasset before he was married and had located the farm in North Parsonsfield. Hardy spent a great part of his winters making logging sleds and oxen yokes, which became famous in this part of the country. Hardy taught Wilbur at a very early age the use of tools, which has always been a valuable asset in his career.

Nearly a year after Wilbur was born, his father was in a railroad accident; and because of back injuries, Mr. Merrill was somewhat incapacitated as long as he lived. Even though these injuries bothered him constantly, he took an active part in town affairs, serving in various capacities such as selectman, town clerk, and mail carrier.

Wilbur's early education was acquired in a one-room schoolhouse about 200 yards from his home. When he was four years old, he moved to the village of East Parsonsfield, and this was his home until he graduated from The University of Maine in 1900.

In 1889, when Wilbur was nine years old, his great grandfather, a captain of the War of 1812, died at the ripe age of ninety-four. Due to his influences on Wilbur, much of the early history of the pioneers, their method of living and customs were passed directly to him.

Although Wilbur was born during the presidential term of Rutherford B. Hayes, the first presidential campaign that he remembers was the race and victory of the democrats, Grover Cleveland and Hendricks. The big campaign banners that were stretched across the highways in North and East Parsonsfield, and in Kezar Falls, with the pictures of the candidates, were wonderful targets for sling shots and stone throwing.

Wilbur's parents were very religious and insisted that he attend church three times every Sunday. In the morning he attended the Quaker Church; the afternoon meeting was at the Baptist Church, and the evening service was with the Bullockites. It was at that time that he arrived at the conclusion that he had enough religion to last him a lifetime. Consequently, he attended church only a few times during his married life. However, he was always liberal in contributions to both Protestant and Catholic Churches.

One of the first pranks that he relates is the episode of his first low-wheeled bicycle, known as a "Safety." (Other bicycles of the time were made of one big wheel and one little wheel.)

"Because of sickness on a certain Sunday morning, Wilbur was unable to attend church with his father and mother. However, shortly after the service began, his mother recognized the bell on his bicycle. He had suddenly recovered and had started riding the new bicycle. Although he undressed and went to bed before the service was out, it had no effect on his mother; and his new bike was stored in the garret for two weeks."

One of his greatest pleasures was attending the country fairs in this section with his father, who, for many years, had several trotting and pacing horses; Wilbur's principal job was in leading the horses to cool them off after each heat, and also to sleep on the bales of straw in order to watch the horses at night. His father always kept him supplied with at least one pair of steer calves. His complete sled and yoke equipment provided great fun for the neighborhood boys; and of course, swimming and fishing in Long Pond was at least a semi-weekly jaunt.

After graduation from the grade school, he attended Parsonsfield Seminary, which at that time offered a three-year course. His course covered English grammar, Latin, Greek, plane and solid Geometry, Algebra, plane Trigonometry, and one term of Calculus. Geology and similar subjects were optional. He attended high school from 1893 to 1896.

His transportation during the winter months was by sled dog. Wilbur, weighing only 110 pounds, made transportation an easy task for his large Newfoundland.

His hobbies as a boy consisted of making sleds, wagons, harness equipment for his Newfoundland dog, fishing in nearby brooks and ponds, making waterwheels for the brooks, and riding his bicycle. His pet peeve as a boy was that he hated carrots and Irish tenors.

During his summers and vacations in high school, he worked for my grandfather, Joseph Merrill Lord, helping to complete the Ossipee Valley Telephone and Telegraph Company's Lines.

In the fall of 1896, Wilbur was enrolled as a freshman at The University of Maine in Orono, Maine. During his freshman year, Bill was assigned the task of keeping the class numerals on the college standpipe. He spent one night in the Orono jail when the one-man police force of that town accused Bill of obstructing traffic. Upon hearing the arm of the law give the order to move on, 120 pound Bill became resentful and refused. He wanted to know why; he soon found out. And Bill still retains this characteristic fearlessness today.

While in his senior year at college, he became of voting age. At this time his father told him that the whole Merrill Clan was Democratic. His father told him not to make the same mistake that the rest of the family had made but to vote the straight Republican ticket. Wilbur argued with his father, "If your advice is so good, why don't you vote Republican?" Wilbur didn't know that changing party loyalty at that time was practically "hari-kari." He has been a staunch Republican, anti-New Dealer, and anti-Square Dealer ever since.

During his senior year, he wrote letters to several electrical concerns; liking the reply from General Electric best, he took a job with that company in the construction department of its Boston office. While at this office, he was sent to the town of Millinocket to help with the electrical installation of the Great Northern Paper Company.

In May, 1901, he was transferred to Schenectady, NY, to take the famous Engineering Students' Testing Course. After working and studying a year in this course, he was loaned to the Hudson River Power Company, which was building a large power plant on the Hudson River at Spire Falls, NY. This loan was probably due to the requests from the power company for technical supervision and help in building a plant. When this was completed, he stayed with the power company as chief operator until the crew was accustomed to handling the equipment. He was then transferred back to the testing department in Schenectady, NY and given charge of the transformer test. After a year, he then transferred to the apparatus department in the section known as Marine Engineering.

In 1904 he was spending his vacation with his parents in East Parsonsfield. While taking a horse and buggy ride to North Parsonsfield, they passed a cider mill and decided to have a drink of good new cider. No one was around, so they helped themselves. They discovered when they got home that the family which operated the mill were all quarantined with scarlet fever. The Board of Health had neglected to put a sign on the mill.

In due time after he returned to Schenectady, he came down with the fever; the doctor recommended Clara Greason, a trained nurse, to care for him. She arrived shortly and did a very efficient job. Wilbur and Clara became engaged during this period.

The wedding was the next June in 1905. In 1906, Mildred, their only child was born. She lived to be twelve years old and died in an automobile accident.

Clara then turned her ambitions to making woven baskets, and sold about $500.00 worth, mostly for the benefit of the Red Cross. After weaving baskets for a few years, she decided to hook rugs. She dyed her own materials and used natural flowers as a pattern for her rugs. She made nearly sixty rugs of various sizes, which in turn took many prizes. Her next hobby was weaving. She wove approximately 800 yards of fine linen towels, table covers, bureau scarfs, all in very intricate designs.

Clara, not satisfied to sit back and relax, decided in the 1920's to raise money enough to buy land in Wilmington, NY, and build a community house for youngsters. She had one helper and together they ran this recreational center for local youngsters. Movies were looked forward to twice a week, and there was dancing once a week. Boating and swimming facilities were also available. Wilbur would go 150 miles up to the camp Friday night and return to Schenectady on Monday morning. At the end of fifteen years, it seemed that all the youngsters had grown up and there were no new ones to take their place, so Clara sold the property to a Fish and Gun Club.

Clara passed away in 1953, after living eight years at Maple Rock Farm.

While he was in Schenectady, Wilbur's Yankee Ingenuity was immediately put to work to solve electrical problems for the electrical equipment then being used in Theodore Roosevelt's program. This included changing practically all of the operation on board ship from steam to electrical operation, such as gun-pointing, turret-turning, ventilation, munition hoists, anchor hoists and water-tight emergency operation. His contribution to this was adopted and put into operation on practically all ships being built at that time.

To indicate the delicacy of control in gun-pointing for instance, the gun could be trained on a ship a mile away with each ship going in opposite directions at full speed, or both going in the same direction at less than a mile's difference in speed. To show the range of control, it could be trained on the sun in the morning and still theoretically be trained on the sun at sunset.

Other contributions that Bill made to the world were the electrical towing system and electrical signaling system, but both are of minor importance.

However, his development of the water-tight (bunker) door, which could be controlled from several parts of the ship by push buttons and automatically close all the doors and divide the ship into many independent sections, was of great importance to war ships. When necessary, a man could raise the doors by electrical control, pass through the door, and immediately it would close again. This was adopted on many ships.

After several years in this department, he was given charge of an engineering section in the apparatus department, and he was responsible for the engineering and developmental work for paper mills, cement mills, printing establishments, including newsprint machinery, quarries, sawmill and lumbering operations, and various minor industries. His contribution to most of these, such as newsprint, paper, cement manufacture, and sawmill equipment, especially in the Northwest, were and still are contributing many millions of dollars annually to the General Electric Company and the industry at large, as most of these patents have long ago expired.

One important contribution which was developed for another purpose resulted in the micro-leveling of high speed elevators, without which our tall buildings, offices and hotels would not have been possible. With the old methods, there was a limit to the number of stories that could be served. Since then, more stories have been added. Previously, practically all the space of the lower stories would have to be taken up by elevator shafts.

Many new problems were proposed to him, and he became known throughout the organization as "Mr. Ingenious Yankee."

The Merrill's wanted birds to visit their garden, and they did everything possible to bring them in. (The year before a pair of woodcock had nested there, something unheard of in Schenectady.) Bill decided that more birds would be attracted to his garden if he had a brook or pool in it. So he took upon himself the task of building a brook - one that would not flow outside the garden, tax the city water supply, or place undue burden on his pocketbook.

Down at the low side of his garden, he sank an old varnish kettle into the ground and walled it up with stones to simulate a natural pool about five feet in diameter to prevent loss of water into the ground. From this pool, he brought a small pipe to an adjacent "pumping station," a small box buried beside the pool and containing a tiny pump and a 12 watt motor. Away from the pump ran a little lead pipe, up the slope to a convincing "spring" in a high corner of the garden.

The "brook" itself was a little series of cascades from the spring to the pool. Each step in the cascade was a rectangular metal trough, each trough of different length. As with the pool and the spring, the underlying artificiality is camouflaged with stones and pebbles, not to mention moss and other attributes of a natural stream.

Among the most important problems was the production of anchor chain for Navy, Merchant Marine, and Allies, prior to World War I. He developed the method of casting the chain in 15 ton batches from electric furnaces and was appointed from Washington to head the organization to put this into production. Chairman of a committee, which consisted of representatives from the American and English Navies, Merchant Marine, Lloyd's of London, and various foundry organizations, he carried through this project to a very successful conclusion, and practically all anchor chain used in larger sizes is being made by this method. This method was used for the chain of the USS *FORRESTAL*.

He held this position until 1925. At that time a new department was established in the Schenectady plant, known as the Works Laboratory Plant, which among other things controlled the specification for all purchase materials and acceptance test of the material. In addition to this, the Works Laboratory Plant was given a free hand in the development of new products. This department started with four engineers, a draftsman, a secretary, and an assistant. When he left this department, it had grown to 300 employees, mostly technicians. About one third of the force was engaged in the development of materials/necessities for the first jet propulsion engine.

Bill was responsible for many of the needed improvements for successful factory operation and originated the first all steel cabinet refrigerators, the electric food disposal, known as the electric pig, and as well as patents which put the operation of the electric dishwasher on an automatic instead of a hand operated basis.

One of the outstanding developments was the erection, installation, and distribution of all gases used in the plant. The combined manufacture of liquid air, oxygen, hydrogen and helium was done in a plant away from the Works Laboratory in order to lessen the dangers of explosion; these gases were then conveyed to the Works Laboratory by means of pipes to put the facilities within reach of every workman that needed this for his duties. This, as opposed to the prevailing method of buying tank gas, credited the laboratory with at least a million dollars savings per year.

Another outstanding development was the method for removing the oxides of what is known as bullring copper. This had always been done by the chemical process of heating thousands of tons of copper rods several times and then plunging them into acid. This removed 10% of the weight which was flushed down the sewer. For 30 years, all copper mills that made drawn copper had been trying to make this a continuous process. This was successfully developed in the Works Laboratory. The 10% was saved, melted and again made into copper wire. It is now a universal method in the whole industry, and the laboratory was credited with another million dollars savings a year.

Nearly every scientific problem that Wilbur tackled, he solved. The only problem not solved during his forty-five years of service with the General Electric Company was at the close of his service. When he retired in 1945, a large section was working on materials for the jet engine. Not only the General Electric Company, but every other concern, including the armed services, were working on materials that would stand higher temperatures as a slight increase in operating temperatures materially increases the power output in any jet engine.

At the time of his retirement, a farewell party was given in his honor. At this time, he received a silver tea service which paid respect to him for designing the first steel cabinets in refrigerators. On the tray was inscribed, "A tribute to Wilbur L. Merrill on the 15th anniversary of his development and production of the all steel refrigerator cabinet from his General Electric business associates. In grateful acknowledgment of his genius and vision."

After retiring, and returning to Parsonsfield, his mechanical mind was still at work figuring distances. In Schenectady, he found that it was two and two-tenths miles from his residence to his office. It was two and two-tenths miles from Mr. Lord's residence to the Merrill residence where he was born.

Once while working with the Marion Steam Shovel Company, he was domiciled at the Marion City Club in Marion, Ohio. One of his many pleasures was having cocktails with his friends after work. While at the Club, he demanded Saratoga Vichy for his highballs. He then discovered that it was not available, and on his return to Schenectady, he sent a case to the club. In 1951, he was having a few cocktails with some of his old friends at the Schenectady City Club, and at a table behind him were two engineers, one from General Electric and one from Marion. Wilbur overheard the Marion engineer saying, "I see you serve Saratoga

Vichy here. We always serve it at the Marion Club. The story behind this is that forty or fifty years ago, a young pipsqueek from Schenectady objected to anything except Vichy, which we did not have. After the club sampled Wilbur's gift, they have used it ever since."

Uncle Wilbur believed that the extensive development of radio and instantaneous transmission around the world is responsible for our present day deplorable conditions. If communication to Russia, China, and other countries had to go by boat or be paid for at commercial rates, both they and the heads of other governments would have time to cool off and come up with more sensible answers. As long as we have radio, we will have war. This, plus other philosophies, was more or less founded by his quite extensive travels for his company to every state in the Union, Alaska, Mexico, Cuba, England, Scotland, France, Italy, Belgium, Canada, Switzerland, Austria, Nova Scotia, Germany, and Holland.

It has, indeed, been a pleasure and a privilege to live with Uncle Wilbur for the past ten years, he has influenced my own mechanical ability as well as giving me the idea for my life's work, and encouraging me in striving for high ideals.

YANKEE INGENUITY IN ENGINEERING

W. L. Merrill, Engineer
Works Laboratory General Electric Company
Paper given before ASME
Nov 29 - Dec 3, 1943

I realize, in presenting a paper before this body, which represents the acknowledged cream of the profession, that you are accustomed to charts and diagrams, and that your training is such that your impressions are more highly developed through the eyes than the ears. Therefore, since I have not developed the art of public speaking beyond the preliminary training period, I have had some charts prepared to clarify my attempt to present this subject. I shall use what ingenuity I have not to detain you too long. (1st slide) "Private Buck" I like to think of an engineer as one who takes materials and processes of nature and adapts them to the security, welfare and happiness of mankind.

Following this formula, we should include in engineering, research. (2nd slide) "Research"

Too much common everyday engineering, development and the like are now called research which should not have the dignity of that term. I like to think of fundamental research as the search for and discovery of new facts and unknown laws of nature. Engineering appears in the picture by taking these fundamentals and applying them to the man's welfare. In this process, Yankee Ingenuity is what makes the whole thing click.

I believe it originates from two sources. First, the environment of the early settlers forced them to exercise a tremendous amount of Yankee Ingenuity or starve. Second, I think it is more or less hereditary. From whatever source it originated, it is certainly one of these bases of our present industrial empire. I would for good measure throw in a possible third source which is ever present desire to lighten a man's own burden possibly a remote cousin to laziness, shaded a little by a desire for praise from his friends.

On the seven seas and on the shores, American forces are known as "Yanks" regardless of race, color, or creed, so Yankee Ingenuity has become known as a National symbol, not tied specifically to the original Yankees. Before our boys get through with the mess on the far flung fronts, Yankee Ingenuity will have an International meaning.

I can think of no more ingenious method for mass production that the testing for hardness and roundness of millions of balls used in ball bearings than bouncing and rolling them on steel plates.

The old shot tower is another good example. I say that the engineers who constructed the first shot tower perhaps knew very little about surface tension.

The calculation and design of a large suspension bridge, like the San Francisco, is an engineering problem. However, the equipment for automatically stranding the wires, each of definite tension into the large cables I would place under the heading of Yankee Ingenuity.

An example with which I was associated displays some Yankee Ingenuity. A number of years ago we had the assignment of developing the all steel refrigerator to supersede wood. It was decided that we should have a nice white porcelain lining and that the outside should be lacquered white to appeal to the housewife's sanitary instincts. We discovered, however, that white was not white, and that where the outside lacquer approached the porcelain inner liner, the difference in the two whites was distressing. Different materials, different whites. A strip of insulating material was necessary to join these two surfaces. White Insulation was tried. Different material, different finish, different white. We now had three instead of two. It looked terrible. I tried out a sample by painting the white strip black. This not only did the trick, but camouflaged the difference between the outside lacquer and the inside enamel. All blended beautifully. Millions of refrigerators and ice boxes having been built since using this black strip framework. I doubt if many manufacturers today even know why they are using black strips. In reading through some old patents granted in the 50's, I came across a patent with claims on the breech and firing mechanism, something as follows:

"I claim first a looseness in all pivoted and sliding parts. This first allows the mechanism to work easily; second, avoids jamming when rusted; third, that the soldier can put more tallow in the joints and moving parts, and the more tallow encased, the less often does he have to grease his gun mechanism.

One of the most outstanding examples of Yankee Ingenuity is the hull and sail design of the famous Yankee clippers. As everyone familiar with sailing vessel history knows, these were very radical, upsetting all previous conceptions of ship design.

I will show one of the recent developments in the shaving of copper rod to produce bull-ring copper. In the production of copper wire, the ingot is poured, approximately 200 lbs. in an iron mold. In cooling, the outside of the ingot is oxidized for a perceptible distance. This ingot is then rolled into bars, say, 3/4" in diameter. It is then ready for the wire mill, but before these bars can be drawn down to small sizes of wire, the concentric ring of oxide silvers, etc. have to be removed. For something over 30 years, this was done by heating the wire bars in open atmosphere to oxidize the surface. They were then pickled and again heated. This expensive process was repeated until practically all the outside ring of oxide was removed, something like 7 or 8 percent of the weight of the bar. For thirty years, fabricators worked on various schemes to remove this mechanically, with varying degrees of success. There was developed in my company a continuous process whereby the original bars were fed through dies to reduce diameter and smooth the surface, then continuously fed through a shaving die which removed the oxide and scale. This is practically no different from the thirty years' unsuccessful trials, with one exception. It would be natural to make a shaving die with a cutting edge clear around the bar, thus when the chip started, in order to clear the die, it had to assume a conical shape. This meant that it had to split somewhere to clear the die. When the chip would split, the bar, being relieved at that point, would crowd towards this side of the die, and the removed portions would become eccentric, and hence leave one side of the bar with oxide still on. The Yankee Ingenuity in this job was to grid a number of faces on the front of the die so that while the cut around the bar was continuous, there were six separate shavings, each of a uniform width. It was realized that in our present emergency great quantities of copper wire have to be produced some 1 and 2 mils thick, and that you cannot have silvers and oxides in bar from which it is drawn. My company at the present time is shaving over a million pounds of copper per week by this method and many of our fabricators are using the same equipment. I am citing this to show that it took at least thirty years before Yankee Ingenuity was put into this process to make it click.

I have attempted to show that there is a very definite connection between ingenuity and engineering. Engineering development and design along established lines will yield a sound product, but for the new short cuts to save labor and material, the new stunt which makes the product radically better, the new scheme which makes possible the heretofore impossible, we must look to Yankee Ingenuity. In engineering training plus Yankee Ingenuity, we have an unbeatable combination.

In industry more attention should be paid to the engineers that show this characteristic. Often a very valuable man to any organization due to this characteristic, is overlooked because of his so-called executive ability and is pigeon-holed in some department for that reason. He should be singled out and given an opportunity of working in close association with others, this ingenuity will bear fruit many-fold.

The seeking of this should be one of the first duties of the head of an engineering department as new men are taken into an organization.

Our technical colleges are providing excellent engineering training, but are they developing Yankee Ingenuity? - I think only subconsciously.

Since it seems so obvious that the trait of Yankee Ingenuity has been and is playing such a part in engineering, and since it is something that cannot be taught to a student any more than music if it is not inherent in the student himself, provision should be made in all our engineering courses to discover and develop students having the ability.

I therefore propose that Yankee Ingenuity have a recognized place in all engineering curricula and that it be designated as YI, following the precedent of IQ.

July 4, 1942

Several of the chaps have asked me to give them the story that I related yesterday at the very enjoyable occasion at the Mohawk Club. It was about as follows: I spent my early days with my grandparents on a farm in Maine.

Grandfather had an old horse; I believe his name was Charlie. He was long past his usefulness and for several seasons he spent his summers in lush pastures and was given excellent care in the barn during the winters with no duties except to eat, drink, and sleep.

Finally, he accumulated so many spavins, heaves, hives, etc. that grandfather thought his suffering was too great and decided to put him out of his misery. Finally, the day was set when he was to be shot. The day before, however, grandfather led him to a neighboring blacksmith's shop and had a brand new set of shoes fitted all around for the occasion.

The shoes did not do Charlie much good for long, but it was great publicity, as we would say today, for grandfather and the blacksmith. - *W L Merrill*

June 13, 1945

During the past 45 years I have traveled in every state in the Union and have flown over 36. I have traveled to and in Mexico, Cuba, Canada, Nova Scotia, England, Scotland, France, Italy, Switzerland, Austria, Germany, Belgian and Holland.

I have traveled by stage, horse car, bus, auto, ferry, taxi, tramp steamer, palatial ocean liner, plane, amphibian, cog-railway, horseback, and private yacht.

I have put up at first, second, third, and four class hotels, boarding houses, rooming houses, private families, YMCAs, dormitories and have even slept on a park bench.

All at the specific request and expense of the General Electric Company.

Have had one expense account returned during World War I for further details. Who in hell says I am not a good accountant? - *Bill Merrill*

An Introduction...

Gentlemen and Scholars:

It is altogether fitting and proper to assemble here with a single purpose - to honor one who has already tasted the fruits of success.

To him who hath it shall be given, and therein lies his hope for the future. But before we follow the general mob, let us look into the past. Some years ago, where the moose abound on the frontiers of our nation, a very small man/child was found on a backwoods Maine plantation.

He may have been born for all we know but anyway he appeared; he learned to cuss, plow and sow without being carefully reared.

As time passed by he grew in girth but mostly in his hair and being close to mother earth he was anything but fair.

In time he grew to man's estate and forsook the backwoods life for the broad green lawns of campus great and the usual college strife.

To claim he acquired some knowledge is putting it rather mildly. For when he left that college he still looked pretty wild.

From that day forth, he was on his own and he started on the run. For what he had reaped, he had also sown, he landed in Boston.

But that old town couldn't hold him, as you can plainly see, he had too damn much vim and landed in Schenectady. From then on, to the present day he's raised particular hell. In many different ways, it's up to him to tell.

At times, he's a bit on the queer side, and attempts to be real tough, but underneath his delicate hide - he's a diamond in the rough.

His good wife calls him Wilbur, but the boys all call him Bill, with never a thought of - dear sir -because it doesn't suit his will.

But from now on, through the ages it is decreed by the sages, from the backwoods up in Maine, that the man we've known and loved so long is no longer sane.

He's taken on a polish, he's drawn into his shell, and the man we knew well as Bill has just gone to plain hell.

They call him Doctor Merrill now but underneath his hide he's just the same old Bill we always used to chide. DR. WILBUR LORIN MERRILL - STAND UP

The brain trust ruled with an iron hand that most of the pigs in our fair land, should never have been born and now must die to keep a right balance twixt demand and supply.

It left a void they never did see, this pigless world could never be. What could be done with trash and bone from tables of the American home. A machine was needed to do the chore, these little pigs had performed before. The great white father, whose name was Swope, thought of Bill Merrill before he wrote.

Take a Muir, with a copy to all those guys in Schenectady, we'll hit the damn ball. He'll give us a machine to do the darn job, or, my name ain't Swope, nor am I called Bob.

The results we all know - it's history now. The Electrical Pig was born without Sow, For such a result it seems fitting to say, Bill Merrill becomes Doctor the easiest way.

MORAL: NEVER TAKE LIBERTIES WITH NATURE IF YOU ARE TO PRESERVE YOUR WAIST LINE.

ELISHA WADLEIGH.

Adapted from *A History of the First Century of the Town of Parsonsfield, Maine, Incorporated Aug 29, 1785*. Portland, Me.: Brown Thurston & Company, 1888.

Elisha Wadleigh, Sr. (F) (b. February 15, 1769 d. July 3, 1872) was born in a garrison house in Kittery, Maine and died in Parsonsfield, Maine.

His parents were too poor to bestow on the son anything outside of existence, and therefore, in those early and troublous times, with father in the War of the Revolution and the struggle great for sufficient subsistence to keep body and soul companions, his education and advantages were none, attending school but one day in his life. After attaining his majority, he married Miss Sally Smith of Berwick, and removed to the town of Parsonsfield as early as 1798-9, and took up a farm (Maple Rock Farm) subject to all the inconveniences and hardships of those early days. Inured to hard work and hard fare, with a physical endowment the envy of ordinary men, jovial and happy, determined and resolute withal, he met the privations and endured the hardships with a manly zeal and spirit, and with his good wife gallantry bore the full share of all the toils and burdens of pioneer life. His political affiliations were from the earliest with the Democratic Party, voting that ticket for over 75 years.

He retained his mental faculties to a wonderful degree. In the last year of his advanced life his memory of early events was keen and accurate. Always easy in conversation, he retained that faculty till the last. Despite the circumstances attendant upon his life, his attainments were fair, reading considerable and retaining what he read. His family was of seven children, four sons and three daughters, all are gone save one, the youngest, Mrs. Catherine Wedgewood, of Newport, Maine.

Elisha Wadleigh Jr. (F) (b. September 15, 1801 d. 1875) Son of Elisha and Sally Smith Wadleigh was born in Parsonsfield, and resided on the farm where he was born until he was " gathered to his fathers" at the ripe age of seventy-four years.

In early life he became a member of the Freewill Baptist Church, and about 1840 was installed deacon, which office and position he filled until his death.

He married Miss Mary, daughter of Caleb Burbank, of Parsonsfield, who survived him but a few years. Three sons and a daughter were the fruit of this union. He was hospitable in the extreme, his home and heart were ever open, cordial and pleasant, always recognizing the source from which flowed all his blessings; love, reverence and thankfulness not only making their impress upon the man and beaming from his Countenance, but in turn making their impress upon those with whom he associated. He was a man of sound judgment and discretion, one of the best of the townsmen, citizens and neighbors; a husband ever faithful; a father indulgent, exemplary, kind and generous; a son whose duty to his aged parents was always performed as a service of love and a noble Christian, to whom the precepts of His Holy Word, governing and controlling his life, were not a grievous burden but a joyous service.

Elisha S Wadleigh

<u>Elisha Smith Wadleigh</u> (F) (b. December 6, 1830 d. June 26, 1912) Son of Elisha, Jr and Mary Burbank Wadleigh, occupies the old homestead, on which Elisha Wadleigh, Sr. settled during the last years of the 1700's. He is one of the prominent farmers and successful businessmen of the town. He has, within a few years, remodeled and enlarged the farmhouse and buildings, planted shade trees, grading and making attractive and pleasant the grounds. It is here his life has been thus far passed, a large part of which has been devoted to caring tenderly for the aged grandparents, and later the father and mother, reaping the reward of pecuniary blessings in addition to the greater, of duty faithfully done, and it is here he intends to pass the remainder of his years. During the past thirty years, he has served on the board of superintending the school committee of the town - twelve years, and was, as several times before, its chairman. He married Mrs. Josephine Lord, July 3, 1879.

182.

THOMAS[6] CHURCHILL (Ichabod,[5] Thomas,[4] Barnabas, Joseph,[2] John[1]). Born in Parsonsfield, Me., Jan. 20, 1798, and lived there. A farmer. Married 1st, at Parsonsfield, Me., March 14, 1830, Mary Banks, born July 9, 1806; married by Rev. John Buzzell. Married 2d, Mrs. Olive B. Roberts, of Whitestown, N.Y.

Children born in Parsonsfield.

432   I. Thomas S.,[7] b. May 6, 1831; m. Mary A. Dixon, Jan. 1, 1855. She was born Oct. 2, 1833.

433   II. Otis B.,[7] b. Nov. 5, 1832; m. Susan E. Ferrin, Jan. 2, 1861; b. Jan. 14, 1839.

434   III. John C.,[7] b. Dec. 11, 1834; m. Annie Burk, Oct. 18, 1869.

    IV. Mary Reliance,[7] b. Feb. 12, 1837; m. Nehemiah T. Libby, Feb. 23, 1860.

Children.

1. Emma A. Libby, b. Nov. 2, 1862.
2. Walter D. Libby, b. Nov. 8, 1864.

    V. Nathaniel,[7] b. May 8, 1839; unmarried.

    VI. Elizabeth A.,[7] b. March 15, 1841; d. March 17, 1844.

    VII. Joseph,[7] b. 1843; d. Oct. 18, 1844.

    VIII. Lydia F.,[7] b. March 15, 1851; m. John Colcord, of Cornish, Me., May 5, 1880.

Child.

1. Lura M. Colcord, b. Aug. 31, 1882.

MAJ. THOMAS CHURCHILL.

MRS. MARY E. CHURCHILL.

3RD DUKE OF SUMMERSET

RES OF THE LATE MAJOR THOMAS CHURCHILL NORTH PARSONSFIELD, ME.

PHYLLIS EVELYN LORD TREWORGY

Obituary

GORHAM - Phyllis Lord Treworgy, 93, died Dec. 30, 2002 at the Maine Medical Center after a brief ill-ness. Phyllis Evelyn Lord Treworgy was born May 27, 1909 at Maple Rock Farm in Parsonsfield. She was the daughter of Joseph Merrill Lord and Sarah Churchill Lord, the youngest of five children. She attended school in Parsonsfield and graduated Parsonsfield Seminary in 1927. She earned a degree from the business course of Nasson Institute in Springvale in 1929. Phyllis moved to Gorham in 1929 to work at Gorham Normal School. While she was living in Gorham, she met and married Audway S. 'Stubby' Treworgy in 1936. They moved to the farm on Flaggy Meadow Road in 1941, where she lived until her death. While at the college, she worked as bursar and secretary to principals Dr. Walter E. Russell and Dr. Francis L. Bailey until 1942, when she and her husband had the first of three children. While raising her family she worked as bookkeeper and secretary to the first superintendent of schools in Gorham from 1955-56. After retiring, Phyllis and Stubby wintered in St. Petersbury, Fla., for 25 years.

Phyllis was a member of the First Parish Congregational Church as well as the Pine Tree Chapter of the Order of the Eastern Star, and the Gorham Garden Club for over 60 years. She was a member of the Gorham PTA, the Gorham Historical Society, the Gorham Extension Service, a ten year member of the Campfire Council and an associate member of the University of Southern Maine Retired Teachers Association. She was care giver to several friends and relatives and was active in the Gorham community for over 73 years.

She greatly enjoyed the company of her children, grandchildren and great-grandchildren and was at her best with a house full of people. She spent many hours playing games and laughing with her family and friends and was renowned for her kindness, generosity, ever-open door, positive attitude, hot milk sponge cake, seafood casserole, and her famous zucchini relish. She had more colorful expressions "than Heinz has pickles". When she was not cooking delicious meals for her family and many visitors, she loved to read novels, do crossword puzzles, knit dishcloths, and crochet afghans for all her children and grandchildren.

Phyllis' home was host to her annual family reunion for 53 consecutive years, an event which could draw as many as 100 relatives from across the country. She was dearly loved by both friends and relatives, and will be greatly missed. She made a difference in every life that she touched.

She was predeceased by her husband of 63 years, Audway S. Treworgy in 1999.

She is survived by her three children, Linda T. Faatz, Martha T. Harris, both of Gorham, and John S. Treworgy and his wife Cheryl of Merrimac, Mass.; ten grandchildren, Robyn Pettengill of Westbrook, Sarah Treworgy and husband, John de LaChapelle of Seattle, Wash., Jennifer P. Banks and husband, Jay Banks of Gorham, Hannah Treworgy of Boston, Mass., Nathan Faatz and wife, Corey of Limerick, Justin Faatz of Boston, Mass., Samantha Treworgy at Smith College in Northampton, Mass., Adam Treworgy at Washington University in St. Louis, Mo., Shalane Flanagan at UNC at Chapel Hill, N.C., Maggie Flanagan at CU at Boulder, Colo.; three great-grandchildren, Jackson, Georgia, and Griffin Banks of Gorham; and close family members John, Faith, Ann and Alison Churchill of Berlin, Conn.

A celebration of her life will be held at the First Parish Congregational Church in Gorham, 1 Church Street on Sunday, Jan. 5, at 2:15 p.m. Visiting hours will be before the service in the church's Fellowship Hall at 1 p.m. Rev. David Butler will officiate the service.

In lieu of flowers, the family suggests donations be made to Baxter Memorial Library, 71 South Street, Gorham, Maine 04038 or First Parish Church of Gorham, 1 Church Street, Gorham, Maine 04038.

Arrangements are by Dolby and Dorr Funeral Chapel, Gorham.

Remarks made at her funeral by her son, John Stuart Treworgy

Phyllis Evelyn was born and raised at Maple Rock Farm in Parsonsfield, Maine. She was named after a horse and a dog, and proud of it. (I suppose that's what happens when your siblings are involved in the naming of their baby sister.)

Maple Rock Farm was the center of activities for a host of family and near-family for generations. That is why Mum always told us she was born and brought up in a crowd. She was proud of that, also.

Phyllis, Phil, Aunt Phyllis, Mrs. T, Mum, Nana, all these names were spoken with genuine affection by her family and near-family alike.

For Linda, Martha, and John, these were always very <u>fuzzy</u> distinctions. Mum's embrace reached well beyond the bounds of blood relatives and included her dearest and oldest friends. Many of these friends were known to Linda, Martha and John as 'Aunts and Uncles'. And our relatives include our closest friends and mentors. I'm not real sure of the exact relationship of most of these folks to this day.

Wilber and Orville took their first flight just 5 years before Mum was born and last year Phyllis flew on a jet plane to Seattle to visit her granddaughter. The crank phonograph was brought to market before she was 10 years old and the radio was invented when she was just a child. Three years ago she got on e-mail at Flaggy Meadow Road and it brought tears to her eyes. Phyllis lived 40% of her life before I was even born and she developed many of her dearest friendships during that period.

Her early career at The College touched so many lives and so many of those lives touched ours, those connections still last until this day. Just look around campus, we have: *Upton* Hall, *Doc Russell* Hall, Auntie *Mim Andrews* Hall, Aunt *Esther Wood* Hall, *Edna Dickie* Hall, *Doctor Bailey* Hall, *Ken Brooks* Hall, The *Costello* Center, and more! All named for people Mum counted among her dearest friends. And many of these people Mum cared for in their waning years, just because she could.

Our household, when the three of us were growing up, was always a bevy of friends and family. Mum loved the activity! Our playmates and childhood friends were always welcome and dinnertime often included one or more of each of them. As some of our friends still recall, dinner at the "T's" was not a brief affair. With 7 or more of us around the dining room table, it could be a raucous, hilarious family gathering that would last into the evening. (Mrs. Loveitt, that's why my homework was late)

My birthday is May 26th and Mum's is May 27th. And for years we celebrated together. (I always enjoyed being one day older.) Last birthday Mum gave me a birthday card that opened with the usual complaints about raising a son:

The mess, the noise, the expense, the worry, (what worry?) But on the inside it simply said, "BUT DIDN'T WE HAVE FUN" (Yes Mum, we did).

My Mother was the most positive, optimistic and giving person I have ever known. She always saw the best in everyone she met and told us all about it. Do you know how aggravating that can be when you really want to dislike someone? But Mum showed us, by example, a valuable lesson. Life is to be enjoyed!

This does not mean just play, but to keep your attitude up beat. Enjoy and appreciate your friends and look forward to those who will soon be added to the list. Have fun in all you do. Live life fully and thoroughly.

Phyllis was also known by all her grandchildren for her colorful expressions and sense of humor. Terms such as "driving 'round the dingle" and "heading for the pucker brush" always amused them.

When I was younger and get "all gussied up" to go out *and* if she approved of my appearance, she would remind me I should be careful. As my Uncle Frank would say, it *could* make the "gals snort and paw the air." But if she didn't approve of our "get-up" she would simply comment we looked "wild and wooly and full of fleas."

When I was little, and Mum really wanted my attention she would call out to me using every family name she could muster up, including pet names; "Linda, Martha, John, Ivory, Fluffy!" (This may explain some of my idiosyncratic behavior, thinking my given name just might include the name "Fluffy.") I later dropped the "Fluffy" part when I got to High School… but *she* never did. (I think I inherited the name gene. I call any number of my children by Hannah's name. But, I'll let them sort it out.)

One morning shortly before she died, I visited her at MMC. She greeted me by saying, with great pleasure, that she had seen her angels. "Imagine that," she said, "there were two of them!" She was smiling when she told us. She said that one was ready to carry her away, but the other said "not yet." She was amused by this event, but remarked, "I'll just let them sort it out." Mum then called all of us (children, grandchildren, great grandchildren) to her bedside to say goodbye. (This may have been the unfinished business the angels had been discussing.) She looked beautiful and totally at peace. She was smiling as she watched 15 or more of us in the hospital room visiting with her and each with other. She had her crowd back…Phyllis entertaining her family up to the last hours of her life. (Mum even had a bag of zucchini relish at the foot of her bed for the nurses, cardiologist, hospital staff, and cousins.) She then thanked us all and gave us each our instructions. (I was pleased to have all my children with me this holiday season and they were all able to stay at Nanny's.) She called me to her side and gave me my short list: "John, be sure you folks eat all the food in the fridge and get your stuff out of the attic." She then told me to go home, play games with the kids and make lots of noise. (The Flaggy Meadow house full of laughter was one of her biggest pleasures.)

My one wish is that we all reflect just a little bit of the light that Philly has shined upon us all.
We all love you, Mum.

Phyllis and Stubby Treworgy

Phyllis

by Rick Austin

Eat all the food in the fridge, she said,
As she lay on the hospital bed.
As she smiled calmly,
She seemed to know,
It would soon be,
Her time to go.

She stood taller than I,
At only half my height.
A pillar of strength.
A guiding light.
A mother to many.
And friend to any,
Who would simply stand in her light.

Each time that she met someone new,
It didn't matter what they would do.
As she smiled calmly,
They came to feel,
Welcome, wanted and loved.
Like they were touched,
From above.

She stood taller than I,
At only half my height.
A pillar of strength.
A guiding light.
A mother to many.
And friend to any
Who would simply stand in her light.

When her time came,
She approached it with the same
Calm smile,
Love of life and zest,
When she exclaimed:
"At the next family reunion, I'll be the best dressed!"

She stood taller than I,
At only half my height.
A pillar of strength.
A guiding light.

A mother to many.
And friend to any
Who would simply stand in her light.

Now there's a new angel on the block.
And the other angels are starting to talk.
But as she smiles calmly,
She will make them all feel,
Welcome, wanted and loved.
Like they were touched,
From above.

Note from Robyn Lord Nichols: Rick Austin is my former husband. In the 12 years we were married, he came to adore Phyllis for many reasons. We spent Christmas day with them here in Florida the first couple years after Molly was born, and of course had the family reunion and lake each year to spend time with her. Rick adored her, most especially because she unquestioningly opened her heart to everyone. She was/is still an angel.

Part Three:
Maple Rock Farm

MAPLE ROCK FARM,

MAPLE ROCK FARM c.1799

A BRIEF HISTORY

by David Bower

Known as Maple Rock Farm, the original house was built in 1799 by Elisha Wadleigh (b. February 15, 1769 d. July 3, 1872), son of John & Patience Wadleigh of Kittery. It was a two story 28' x 38' colonial home. Elisha Wadleigh married Sally Smith and had seven children. The oldest son, Deacon Elisha Wadleigh, Jr. (b. September 15, 1801 d. September 15, 1875), inherited the house.

Elisha Jr. married Mary Burbank and they had four children, three sons and a daughter. The oldest son, Elisha Smith Wadleigh (b. December 6, 1830 d. June 26, 1912) inherited the house. Elisha S. married the widow Josephine (Merrill) Lord, daughter of Joseph and Hannah (Burbank) Merrill. Elisha S. remodeled and enlarged the house – in part cutting the house in half horizontally, raising the second floor up to become the third floor and adding the second floor – and planted the maple trees.

Josephine's son, Joseph Merrill Lord, inherited the house. Joseph (b. October 29, 1865 d. February 27, 1920) married Sarah Churchill and they had five children – two daughters and three sons. Joseph practiced law at the house and also started the first telephone company serving the area, the wiring for which was located in what is now the family room. Joseph and Sarah's three sons – Frank, Myron and Daniel Lord – lived on the farm with their families, planted the apple trees and went into the egg business. Maple Rock Farm was a major employer in the area for many years. Wilbur and Clara Merrill, cousins, also lived at the farm for a time. Wilbur Merrill is credited with inventing the "electric pig" a.k.a. the garbage disposal.

Daniel Lord's wife, Irene Stanley, sold the house to Bob and Fritzi (Berger) Russell in 1963. Fritzi was an Olympic figure skater for Austria. She competed against Sonja Henie in the 1928 and 1932 Winter Olympics, taking silver each time to Sonja's gold. Bob Russell, a former banker, wanted to be the apple baron of south-west Maine and purchased many orchards in the Parsonsfield area. He quickly found out that running an orchard was not like running a bank and could not be done from an office.

Bob and Fritzi sold the farm to Tom Saliba in 1975, who, after leasing out the orchard and the buildings for many years, developed the parcel in 1989. The house and outbuildings were not included in the resulting subdivision.

While Maple Rock Farm is the most recognized name, because of the family history, the house is also known as the Wadleigh – Lord house.

Editor's note: Maple Rock Farm is now a wedding venue, owned by John Moody.

Theresa Churchill Lord and Doris Verbeck

FINDING THERESA CHURCHILL LORD'S MAPLE ROCK FARM PHOTOS

by Libby Tucker

Ever since the 1970s, when my grandfather, Don Libby, passed away, I had known that there were Maple Rock Farm photos somewhere in my parents' big house on Alamo Avenue in Colorado Springs. Filled with family memorabilia, the house was full of photo albums, furniture, and dishes that kept the past alive. After my mother passed away in 1994, cousin Linda kept asking, "Aren't there Farm photos in that house somewhere?" I looked, but nothing came to the surface; the house, crammed full of family treasures, did not want to give up the Farm pictures. Like Shirley Jackson's Hill House, it had a mind of its own. But finally, after Dad passed away in 2017, Margie and I sorted through everything in that huge house. I was shocked to discover that the Farm pictures were just a bunch of old, corroded negatives in a brown cardboard folder. Written on the folder, in my Nana's writing, was "Farm pictures. Give to Phyllis." I put the envelope down, then lost it in a welter of other old things. Sad about the loss of our father, Margie and I were finding it hard to focus on the all the things he had left behind. Later Margie, the chief cleaner-upper, found the folder and sent it to me. My husband Geof used his photo expertise to print a few of the negatives, but the negatives were old and badly damaged. Like magic, bits of J. Merrill, his Sarah, and their happy, boisterous children and dogs emerged on the computer screen. Fortunately, Geof found a friend, Dave Williams, who specialized in restoring old photographs, and now we have a complete set of family photos from the early to mid-twentieth century. Thank you, Hill House, for letting us retrieve these important pieces of our family's past!

Elisha Wadleigh and Otis Churchill with Phyllis Evelyn Lord

Annie Eastman

Annie and Charles Eastman

Back: ?, Ray Strout, Myron Lord; middle: Frank Lord, Lena Strout, ?; front: Phyllis Lord

Myron Lord, Doris Verbeck Lord, Frank Lord

Back row: David Lord, Dan Lord, Bobbie Lord, Irene Lord, Myron Lord;
middle row: Wilbur Merrill, Don Libby, Kay Libby, Theresa Libby;
front: Ann Lord, Jose Lord, Howard Lord

Jay Lord

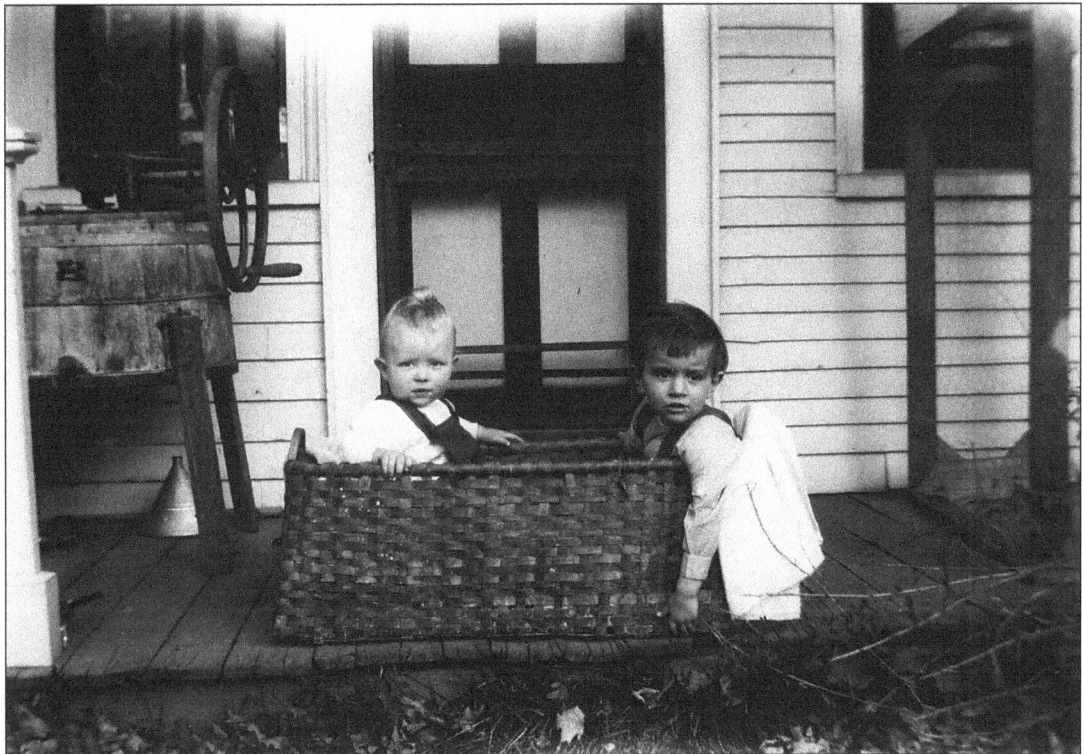

Top: Doris and Jay Lord; bottom: Jay Lord and Leon Kendall

Percival Bott, Frank Lord, Myron Lord

Myron Lord, Theresa Lord, Frank Lord, Percival Bott, Dan Lord, Sarah Lord

Top: Dan, Myron, Frank Lord; Page Illsley, Ray Strout, Randolph

Dan Lord, Don Libby, Frank Lord

Theresa Churchill Lord

Jo Sweeney Lord

Myron Lord

Don Libby

Otis Churchill

Frank Lord

Dan Lord

Myron Lord

Doris Verbeck Lord

Bottom: Dog: Mack Sennet

Top: Myron Lord; bottom: Dan Lord (seated) and farm hands

Top: Dan Lord; bottom: Otis Churchill

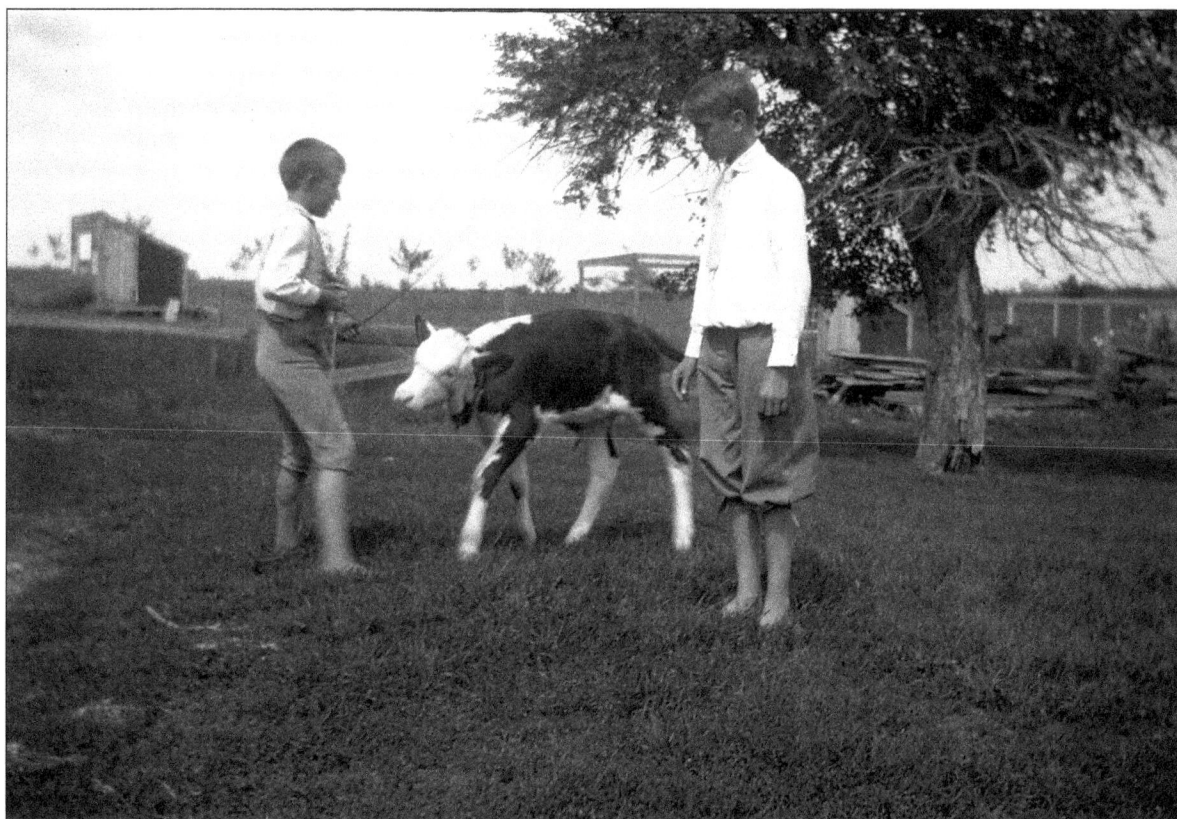

Summer visitors: a lawyer and his family from Boston

Top: J. Merrill Lord on front seat with hat; riders in fancy hats are cousins
Midge and Pet from New York City

1915

Notes

A. The number denotes the generation for that person in that section of the genealogy.

B. Source: Paragraph 1 and 2 from *The History of Nathan Lord Family of Kittery, Maine* by CC & George E Lord – Concord, NH: Rumford Press 1912: pages 1-9, 44-45 and page 90.

C. Source: 162 & Sybil Noyes Notes *Limington Records* page 1 and page 6-8.

D. Source: *Libby Family in America* Daniel's number there 1-6-5.

E. John and his family are all buried in Limington and Cornish about 300 yards on the same side of the road before you get to the Sky Ranch coming down route 117 from Limington.

F. Daniel and Josephine lived in the house later owned by Myron Otis Lord, about one half mile north of the Elisha Wadleigh Farm (also known as Maple Rock Farm). Joseph Merrill Lord and Hattie Julia Lord were both born in this house, where they both lived until their deaths. Hattie Lula Strout, who was orphaned at an early age also lived at the Wadleigh Farm until her marriage to Leon Kendall in 1914. The house that Daniel and Josephine had lived in was next occupied the Reverend Thomas Strout of North Gorham, Maine, who married Rachel Hicks. They had four sons: Frank, Arthur, Horace and Charles. Arthur married Hattie Lord and became the step-father to Hattie Strout. Hattie Lord Strout died in 1890 at Maple Rock Farm and Arthur died in 1893 in San Diego, CA. Frank married Stella Lombard and became a father to Roy, Iza, Mary, Rachel, Raymond and Gordon.

G. John Churchill was a resident of Plymouth, Massachusetts as early as 1643 and was of military age at that time. William Pontus, father of Hannah Pontus was a resident of Plymouth, Massachusetts as early as 1633 and was born in 1623 possibly Holland.

H. Source: *The Churchill Family in America* by Gardner Asaph Churchill and Nathaniel Wiley Churchill. Published by the family of Gardner A. Churchill, 1904.

I. Ichabod Churchill moved to North Parsonsfield, Maine, in 1797 and was the first settler of that name in that town. He lived at the top of what became Churchill Hill in North Parsonsfield, Maine, which was owned by the family for many years. Nathaniel H Churchill was Ichabod's grandson who was the last Churchill family member to own the property. Ichabod was often described as a pushing and prosperous man, who was kind and benevolent but eccentric and notable for his peculiar religious ideas and practices. He believed he was under a special guidance of the Holy Spirit and it is said that he obeyed every impulse promptly without consulting reason.

Index

This is a name-only index for the genealogy section, 1-54. Stories and photos in Parts Two and Three are not indexed.

A

Aigner, Anne-Marie Barbara   8, 23, 41
Aigner-Treworgy, Adam Scott   8, 11, 23, 29, 41, 46
    Samantha Lenard   8, 11, 23, 29, 41, 46
Allen, Leah   16
Anderson, Edna Anise   19, 35
Appleton, Barbara Jane   7, 22, 40
Arsneault, Ruth Sarah   8
Austin, Max Phillip   10, 13, 28, 33, 45, 48
    Molly Lord   10, 13, 28, 33, 45, 48
Austin, Richard Allen   10, 28, 45

B

Bagwell, Andrew Clinton   24, 30, 36, 37
    Julie Renee   24, 30, 36, 37
    Lonnie M   24,36
Banks, Georgia Elizabeth   11, 13, 29, 33, 46, 48
    Griffin William   11, 13, 29, 33, 46, 48
    Jackson Audway   11, 13, 29, 33, 46, 48
    Jay Hudson   11, 13, 29, 33, 46, 48
    Jay Kenneth   11, 29, 46
    Mary Edgecomb   16
Barnett, Ava Magdalene   20, 52
Black, Alexandra Leigh   26, 31, 43, 47
    Carson James   26, 31, 43, 47
    Cheryl Lee   21, 25, 40, 42
    James Fredrick   21, 26, 40, 43
    James Orion   19, 21 38 ,40
    John Carroll   21, 26, 40, 43
    Laura Jane   19, 21, 38, 40
    Verne McAllister   19, 38

Blaisdell, Edythe   18, 50
Blinkhorn, Abby Louise   12, 32, 47
Bliss, Meredith Lynn   26, 43
Bonney, James Hall   7, 22, 41
    Leigh Ann   7, 10, 22, 28, 41, 45
Boothby, Joseph   17, 35
    Lillian R   17, 19, 35
Borisovna, Ludmila   9, 27, 44
Bowen, Elizabeth Ann   11
Burgess, Ronald Dean   12, 32, 48
    Sadira Nadine   12, 14, 32, 34, 48, 49
Burk, Annie   17, 50

C

Chapman, Ida Belle   18, 38
Christofferson, Jill Marie   10, 28, 45
Churchill, Alison Jane   24, 29, 50, 51
    Anne Elizabeth   24, 29, 50, 51
    Barnabas   15
    Barnabas Jr   15
    Cass Randolph   25, 31, 42, 46
    Charles Clarence   17, 18, 38
    Charles Clarence II   19, 21, 38, 39
    Dana Lester   23, 29, 50
    Dawn Linda   21, 25, 39, 42
    Desire   16
    Ebenezer   15
    Eliezer   15
    Elizabeth   16
    Elizabeth Ann   16, 17
    Emma Jean   31, 34, 46, 49
    Eulalie   17, 18, 50

Eva   17, 35
Frank Percy   17, 18, 50
Gamaliel   16
Hannah   15
Harry William   18, 19, 35
Helen May   18, 19, 38
Ichabod   15,16
Isaac   15
John   15, 16
John C   16, 17, 50
John I   16
John II   16
John Preston   20, 24, 50
Joseph   15, 16, 17
Lauren Sarah   23, 29, 50, 51
Lemuel   15
Lindsey Crawford   18, 20, 50
Lindsey Crawford, Jr   20, 23, 50
Lindsey Walter   17,18, 50
Lord Randolph   18, 19, 38
Lydia   15,16
Lydia Frances   16, 17
Lynn Donna   21, 25, 39, 42
Mabel Harriet   19, 21, 35, 36
Margaret   15
Mary Ann   15, 16
Mary Reliance   16, 17, 52
Mercy   15
Nancy   16
Nathaniel   16
Nathaniel H   16, 17
Nicholas   16
Otis Banks   16,17, 38
Polly   16
Preston Banks   17, 18
Robert Alan   21, 25, 39, 42
Robert Winston   19, 21, 38, 39
Ruth Louise   19, 21, 35, 36
Sarah May   5, 17, 18, 38
Spencer Charles   25, 31, 42, 46
Steven Mark   21, 25, 39, 42
Susan Beth   21, 25, 39, 42
Susanna   16
Thomas   15, 16
Thomas (Major)   16

Thomas G   17, 18, 35
Thomas Smith Jr   16,17, 35
Thomas William   19, 20, 35, 36
Wilbur F   17, 18, 38
William   15
William Dennet Dixon   17, 18, 35
Coates, Jason Steven   25, 31, 42, 46
   Steven   25, 42
Colcord, John Washington   17
Colcord, Lura Mildred   17, 19
Compare, Holly Ann   25, 42
Conley, Judith   3
Cox, Katherine Leslie   25, 31, 36, 37
   Michael Lee   25, 36
Crommet, Jennifer Lillian   26, 43
Curtis, Makaila Rayne   30, 34, 36, 37, 49
   Michael Dalton   30, 36

D

Daigle, Renee Sarah   31, 47
Daniels, Florence K   18, 50
Darby, Curley James   30, 54
   Kelly Carolyn   30, 33, 54
   Luke William   30, 33, 54
Davis, Susan Joyce   11, 29, 46
de LaChapelle, Finn Stuart   11, 13, 29, 33, 46, 48
   Jack Edward   11,13, 29, 33, 46, 49
   John   11, 29, 46
Dennis, Adele Lynne   24, 30, 53, 54
   Edwin Lamar Jr   24, 53
   Laura Leigh   24, 30, 53,54
Dixon, Aimee Leigh   9, 12, 27, 32, 44, 48
   Audre Ruth   9, 13, 27, 32, 44, 48
   David Alan   9, 27, 44
   Dianne Lynne   9, 12, 27, 32, 44, 48
   Mary Ann   17, 35
Dodge, Martha Ann   7, 23, 41
Doe, Elizabeth   16
Dopp, Nancy Ruth   21, 39

E

Edgar, Sophia Knapp   17
Edwards, Charlotte   21, 40

Ekwere, George   11, 29, 46
  Jasper Bigelow   11, 13, 29, 33, 46, 49
Emmons, Daniel Robert   31, 34, 47, 49
  Joshua Brian   31, 47
Everett, Martha   3
Ewer, Mary   16

F

Faatz, Anna Elizabeth   11, 13, 28, 33, 45, 48
  Joshua Nicholas   11, 13, 28, 33, 45, 48
  Justin Joshua   7, 11, 23, 28, 41, 45
  Wright Everett   7, 23, 41
Fates, Nathan Andrew   7, 10, 23, 28, 41, 45
  Sophia Sage   10, 13, 28, 33, 45, 48
Ferren, Susan E   17, 38
Flanagan, Maggie Clare   8, 23, 42
  Shalane Grace   8, 23, 42
Forbes, Katie   12, 13
  Alexander   12, 14
  Allison   12, 14
  Andrew   12, 13
  Douglas Burns Jr   12
Francis, Elizabeth Anne   12, 32, 47
Frankel, Dawn   25, 42
Fuller, John C   30, 53

G

Gentleman, Duane Eugene   24, 29, 53
  Edgar Francis   18, 52
  Kathryn Jo   24, 30, 53
  Lawrence B   20, 24, 52, 53
  Lynn Olin   24, 29, 53
  Merton Eugene   18, 20, 52
  Merton Eugene, Jr   20, 24, 52, 53
  Nathan Eugene   29, 33, 53, 54
  Sarah Diane   29, 33, 53, 54
  Sharon Kay   24, 30, 53
Gilpatrick, Rodney Lee   26, 43
Glover, Fred Ingraham   6, 22, 40
Goodwin, Mary   4
Gould, Geoffrey David   8, 26, 43
  Peter Coryell   8, 12, 26, 32, 43, 47
Grabbe, Cody Taylor   30, 33, 53, 54
  David Bruce   30, 53
  Kaylee Brynn   30, 33, 53, 54

Gravino, Shelley   10, 27, 44

H

Harlow, Lydia   15
Harris, Robert Hurlbert   8, 23, 41
Hays, Benjamin Maxwell   9, 12, 27, 32, 44, 47
  Daniel McGowan   6, 9, 22, 27, 40, 44
  David Libby   6, 9, 22, 27, 40, 44
  David Ware   6, 22, 40
  Susan Seabury   6, 9, 22, 26, 40, 43
  Will McGowan   9, 12, 27, 32, 44, 48
Hendershott, Anne Clemens   10, 28, 45
Henderson, Mary Alberta   7, 22, 41
Hicks, Sarah   15
Higgens, Patricia Garland   25, 42
Hubbard, Flora Lillian   19, 52
Hussey, Barbara May   8

I

Ives, Alexis Catherine Jade   25, 31, 42, 47
  Eric Samuel David   25, 31, 42, 47
  Stuart Nicholas Henry   25, 31, 42, 47
  Wayne Christopher   25, 42

J

Jackson, Edgar Porter   19, 35
  Lucille   19, 20, 35
Jepson, Janet Irene   9, 27, 44
Jewell, David Lester   21, 36
Jopp, Nancy   21, 39

K

Kajander, Vieno Mary   20, 50
Kendall, Angela Mae   9, 11, 13, 27, 44
  Constance Louise   8, 12
  Joseph Hussey   8, 9, 11, 27, 44
  Leon Ellsworth   6
  Leon Ellsworth, Jr   6, 8
  Ryan Joseph   9, 11, 13, 27, 44
Kindscher, Allison Kay   30, 33, 53, 54
  James David   30, 53
  Lauren Raissa   30, 33, 53, 54

Klezos, Michael   29, 51
Knight, Olive   4
Knott, Margaret   10, 28, 45

L

Leonard, Dorothy Mae   21, 39
Lester, Roberta Gail   23, 50
Libby, Carleton Glen   19, 20, 52
   Carolyn Lou   20, 24, 52, 53
   Donald Maxwell   5, 19, 39
   Emma A   17,18, 52
   Eunice   5
   Harold Weston   19, 20, 52
   Joanne Elizabeth   5, 6, 19, 22, 39, 40
   Kathryn Churchill   5, 6, 19, 22, 39, 40
   Nehemiah Towle   17, 52
   Sarah Stone   4
   Shirley Jeanne   20, 24, 52, 53
   Walter Day   17, 19, 52
Livernois, Denise   26, 43
Lord, Aaron   4
   Abraham 3
   Abraham (Captain)   3
   Adam   4
   Alan David   7, 10, 22, 28, 41, 45
   Amy   4
   Ann   3, 6, 7, 20, 22, 39, 41
   Anna   4
   Anne   3
   Benjamin   3, 4
   Calvin Ambrose   10,13, 27, 32, 44, 48
   Calvin Merrill   10, 13, 28, 33, 45, 48
   Dana Wadleigh   7, 10, 22, 28, 41, 45
   Daniel   4, 5
   Daniel Bertram   5,6, 18, 20, 38, 39
   David Kimball   7, 10, 23, 28, 41, 45
   David Merrill   6, 7, 20, 23, 39, 41
   Donna Jeanne   7, 9, 11, 22, 27, 40, 44
   Frank Wadleigh   5, 6, 18, 19, 38
   Geoffrey Stacy   7, 9, 22, 27, 40, 44
   George   5
   Harriet Newell   5
   Hattie Julia   5
   Howard Verbeck   6,7, 19, 22, 39, 40

   Jabez   4
   Jacob   4
   James   4, 5
   James (Sargeant)   4
   Jay Merrill   6, 7, 19, 22, 39, 40
   Jay Merrill II   7, 10, 23, 28, 41, 45
   Jeremiah   4
   John   3, 4, 5
   Jonathan Daniel   7, 10, 23, 28, 41, 45
   Jonathan Daniel, Jr   10, 13, 28, 33, 45, 48
   Joseph   4
   Joseph Merrill   5,7, 9,10, 18, 22, 27, 38, 40, 44
   Josieda Marie   9, 13, 27, 32, 44, 48
   Judith   3
   Keziah   4
   Lydia   4
   Margery   3
   Martha   3
   Mary   3, 4
   Meribah   4
   Moses   4
   Myron Otis   5, 6, 18, 20, 38, 39
   Nancy Carol   7, 9, 22, 27, 40, 44
   Nathan   3
   Nathan II   3
   Nathan III   3
   Nathan IV   4
   Olive   5
   Phebe M   5
   Philip Wadleigh   6, 7, 19, 22, 39, 41
   Phyllis Evelyn   5, 6, 18, 20, 38, 39
   Richard   4
   Richard (Captain)   3
   Robyn Jeanne   3, 4, 7, 10, 22, 28, 41, 45
   Samuel   3
   Sarah   3, 4
   Susan Diane   7, 9, 22, 27, 40, 44
   Theresa Churchill   5, 18, 19, 38, 39
   William   3
Love, Frank   24, 53

M

Marston, Marguerite Grace   19, 38
Mauger, Willa-Jo   21, 39

Maynard, Charlotte Louise   24, 53
McCausland, Ellen Douglas   9, 27, 44
McClun, Marie Ona   20, 52
McKenney, Louisa   5
McNeil, Rebecca Joy   31, 46
Merrill, Josephine Burbank   5
Miller, Lilly Anne   12, 32, 34, 47, 49
  Matthew Joseph   12, 32, 47
Mitchell, Andrew Russell   9, 12, 26, 32, 43, 47
  Brian Thomas   9, 12, 26, 32, 43, 47
  Grace Tucker   12, 14, 32, 34, 47, 49
  Jack William   12, 14, 32, 34, 47, 49
  Susan Anne   9, 12, 26, 32, 43, 47
  William Charles Jr   9, 26, 43
Moran, Claire   21, 24, 36
  Jesse Clinton   21, 36
  Julie   21, 24, 36
  Martin Richard   25, 42
  Ruth   21, 24, 36
  Thomas Olin   21, 24, 36
Morrill, Heidi Sinclair   31, 47

N-O

Nichols, Paul Allen   10, 28, 45
Norris, Dorothy Elizabeth   20, 52
Owens, David John   8, 26, 43

P

Paige, Hailey   25, 42
Pedlow, Patricia Cheryl   8, 23, 42
Perkins, Michelle   31, 46
Petrich, Benjamin Clark   30, 33, 54
  Ian Norris   30, 33, 54
  Martin Anthony III   30, 54
Pettingill, Jennifer Lord   8, 11, 23, 29, 41, 46
  Eric Mark   8, 23, 41
  Robyn Dayle   8, 11, 23, 28, 41, 45
Pettit, Kyle Robert   13, 32, 48
Pierie, Elizabeth   31, 46
Pike, Chad Robert   26, 31, 43, 47
  Corey Patricia   10, 28, 45
  David Wyer   21, 26, 40, 43
  Katherine Lee   26, 31, 43, 47
  Lorie Lee   21, 26, 40, 43
  Robert Leroy   21, 40

Pontus, Hannah   15
Powell, Cheryl D   29, 53

Q-R

Rabb, Lucius Raymond   13, 14, 32, 34, 48, 49
  Ronald Raymond Jr   13, 32, 48
  Wyleigh Jay   13,14, 32, 34, 48, 49
Rickard/Reccord, Giles   15
Riggs, Rebecca Catherine   12, 32, 47
Ripley, Susan Holly   9, 27, 44
Ritzaupt, Larry   10, 28, 45
Roberts, Olive Bowers   17, 35
Rogers, Candace   10, 27, 44
  Sarah Rosalind   11, 28, 45
Roghaar, Linda Lou   8, 23, 41
Rossborough, Connie Elizabeth   7, 22, 40
Roth, Anna   9, 27, 44

S

Sargent, Ryan Travis   14
  Ryker Trig   14
Sawyer, Priscilla Ann   10, 28, 45
Scalise, Faith Anne   24, 50
Schmidt, Jack Moulton   30, 54
  Jennifer Libby   30, 34, 54
  Jessica Ingrid   30, 34, 54
  Thomas   25, 42
Seamans, Eric Joseph   25, 31, 42, 46
  Richard Edward   25, 42
Smith, Carolyn Sue   24, 30, 53, 54
  John Bunyan Jr   24, 53
  Sharon Ann   24, 30, 53, 54
Spradley, Helga   24, 36
Stacy, Marilyn Leatrice   7, 22, 40
Stanley, Irene   6, 20, 39
Staples, Randall Mark   12, 32, 48
Stocks, Caleb Andrew   31, 34, 46, 49
  Christopher   25, 31 42, 46
  Dylan Christopher   31, 34, 46, 49
  Isaac Timothy   31, 34, 46, 49
  Jeffrey Allen   25, 31, 42, 46
  Olivia Rosana   31, 34, 46, 49
  Tim   25, 42

Strout, Arthur Louis   5
   Hattie Lula   5, 6
Sturgeon, Andrea Lynn   26, 31, 43, 47
   Maci Jane   31, 34, 47
   Michael David   26, 31, 43, 47
   Reese Caroline   31, 34, 47, 49
   Robert William   26, 43
Sweat, Clara Mabel   18, 35
Sweeney, Edith Josephine   6, 20, 39

T

Tenneson, Lindsey   12, 32, 47
Thiessen, Betty Lou   24, 53
Tozier, Martha   3
Treworgy, Audway Stuart   6, 20, 39
   Hannah Bigelow   8, 11, 23, 29, 41, 46
   John Stuart   6, 8, 20, 23, 39, 41
   Linda   6, 7, 20, 23, 39, 41
   Martha   6, 8, 20, 23, 39, 41
   Sarah Churchill   8, 11, 23, 29, 41, 46
Tucker, Elizabeth Godfrey   6, 8, 22, 26, 40, 43
   Frank Hammond   6, 22, 40
   Margaret Sayre   6, 9, 22, 26, 40, 43
   Sarah Lowell   6, 8, 22, 26, 40, 43

U-V

Underwood, Baxter Donald   12, 14, 32, 34, 48, 49
   Donald Wesley   12, 32, 48
   Gibson David   12, 14, 32, 34, 48, 49
Verbeck, Ruth Doris   6, 19, 39
Violette, Dana   11, 28, 45

W

Wadleigh, Elisha Smith   5
Wang, Wei   29, 51
Weeks, Emily Susan   21, 25, 36
   George Walter   21, 36
   Marshall Wendall   21, 25, 36
Whalen, Daniel James   9, 26, 43
   James David   9, 12, 26, 32, 43, 47
   Thomas Hopkins   9, 12, 26, 32, 43, 47
White, Christopher David   30, 33, 54
   Courtney Lynn Adele   30, 34, 54

White, David Patrick   30, 54
Wiggin, Oscar F   18, 52
Wilson, Christina   24, 30, 36
   Cindy Kay   24, 30, 36
   James Alan   24, 36
   Raymond Elliot   24, 30,36, 37

X-Z

Zeisberg, Shirley Dagmar   10, 28, 45
Zhang, Wayne   29, 51

www.ingramcontent.com/pod-product-compliance
Lightning Source LLC
Chambersburg PA
CBHW041603260326
41914CB00011B/1375